THE SOUTHERN WAY

CONTENTS

© Kevin Robertson (Noodle Books) and the various contributors 2010
ISBN 978-1-906419-32-5
First published in 2010 by Kevin Robertson
under the **NOODLE BOOKS** imprint
PO Box 279
Corhampton
SOUTHAMPTON
SO32 3ZX
www.noodlebooks.co.uk
Printed in England by
Ian Allan Printing Ltd
Hersham, Surrey

A panoramic view of the sidings just beyond Coulsdon North. For many years there were twelve of these and certainly up to 1929 an overhead electric supply was provided for berthing the former LBSCR electric stock. This particular view probably dates from around May 1937 and is from the collection of Derek Taylor, whose Grandfather, John Taylor, worked on the S & T of the Southern Railway and then British Railways from 1927 until retiring in 1972. The date also corresponds with when John Taylor was given a camera as a 30th birthday present. By 1937, the former overhead masts and wires had been removed, replaced by conductor rail on most sidings: were the 'COR' sets in use or pending introduction into service? The coal and timber yard of Messrs. M A Ray is also fascinating, especially the rail access, with each of the sidings on which the wagons are standing being a dead-end.

Derek Taylor

Editorial Introduction

It never ceases to amaze me the breath and width of knowledge that remains seemingly untapped over subjects which many readers will only have known from photographs or the written word.

Just when we might think there can be little else to say about the steam-era railway, someone else comes up with a new discussion topic or is able to answer, or indeed pose, a question no one seems to have previously considered. For proof of this, venture on to any of the numerous e-mail discussion groups, or browse through what can only be described as the learned journals produced by the various pre-grouping support societies. I would not attempt for one moment to put 'Southern Way' into such a collection, but I would add that at times we are asked questions that have so far seemed elusive.

One specifically comes to mind, that of wheel-tappers: with absolutely noting to do with a certain TV programme of the dim and distant past, 'The Wheeltappers and Shunters Social Club - *Affiliated*'. So, did the Southern Railway / Region have such persons as wheeltappers and if so where and how did they work?

I recall seeing photographs and I think some film footage of a wheeltapper at work, but certainly not on the SR. At the time I thought nothing of it, but if they did exist south of the Thames, where on the SR would such men have been employed and if it were at the London Termini how did they manage their task with a conductor rail nearby? (Unless such tasks were carried out at locations such as the sidings at Clapham Junction). Equally, if they did work in the platforms at Waterloo or Victoria it would still mean only one side of a vehicle might be checked. Answers on a post-card please….., seriously, any comments to add to the ever growing minutia of information on our favourite subject would be appreciated.

A question we posed some time ago has also yet to be answered, that of the Southern Railway Museum. Regular readers will recall the stickers shown on the reverse of some prints in the collection clearly indicating as such. We would still love to know if this was simply a paper / photographic record or if it was the start of a well-intended museum project - witness of course the various items of hardware that were also seemingly laid aside at Eastleigh in the 1930s. (Anyone fancy having a stab at some research and an article on the subject?)

Now a comment on one of the articles appearing in this issue, that from Rodney Youngman on his experiences at Winchester, especially in the booking office. In his piece Rodney naturally talks mainly of his own first hand knowledge, wonderfully interspersed with snippets from those who he came across during his career. Indeed, as I have stated in the introduction on page 60, change the location and the stories would probably be very similar at any number of similar sized locations on the SR: and that is in no way intended to be derogatory to Rodney.

What would be good to include in the future would be more behind the scenes stories, the offices at Waterloo, Croydon, Exeter etc. I look forward to what transpires.

Finally from the soapbox, an acknowledgement of the time and effort many of our contributors make in researching and compiling either factual or personal records of the railway. I cannot guarantee the eventual reward will be at the minimum hourly wage, certainly that is if in any way similar to my own perspective. As ever, thanks to all for their continuing support.

Kevin Robertson

Front Cover - *'Lord Nelson' class 4-6-0 No. 30855 'Robert Blake' rounding the curve past Branksome shed heading for the main line, Bournemouth Central and eventually Waterloo.*
David Smith

Rear Cover - *We are often asked for views of station forecourts, like goods yard view, not the easiest to find and certainly not in colour. This image then of the up side frontage at Southampton Central in the early 1960s hopefully fulfils part of the requirement. In the days prior to the opening of the Airport Station and before the demolition of the building seen here from 1965 onwards, a bus shuttle was operated by what was then Southampton Corporation Transport. (I am told by the bus experts that the vehicle is an Albion 'Nimbus'.)*
Howard Butler collection

Opposite - *'No, not Rod Hoyle this time, but it is certainly in his style. We know not who, where or when, but on the reverse of the print was marked a simple, 'For the love of a Bulleid coach'. What more can be said? (Well - something perhaps, keep an eye out for Michael Welch's new 'Southern Coaches in Colour' title, as advertised on the inside cover.)*

'RAILWAY ACCIDENTS AND RELATED INCIDENTS IN DEVON' (*MAINLY*) OR 'THE PERILS OF RAIL TRAVEL A CENTURY OR MORE AGO'

Rod Garner

The subject of railway accidents is a fascinating and yet somewhat uneasy area of interest, generating a slight feeling of guilt in your scribe, as if the story of the misfortune of others is being used as a subject of entertainment for the reader. However it is true to say that whilst the history of accidents on the railways does indeed provide much of interest to the historian and railway enthusiast, it is also true that the development of safety on the railways was driven to a considerable extent by the outcome of investigations into these accidents and the recommendations of the investigating inspectors, and as such is a worthy area of interest.

During earlier research into other matters, I came across a rich source of local reporting of railway-related accidents and incidents which had occurred in Devon (mainly, but not exclusively in the north of the County) over a lengthy period. The wide variety and nature of these incidents, ranging from the minor, and in those days commonplace, accident to the more serious, occasionally humorous and at times bizarre occurrence, brought me back to the archive to extract some details for this article. The details are taken from newspaper reports of the day and thus often and necessarily only give part of the story. In some cases I have been able to delve further and attempted to present a fuller picture. However, the broad spectrum of incidents – not necessarily accidents – related in the press, coupled with the often amusing method of reporting, makes for interesting reading and perhaps throws a little more light on to the daily operation of railways in the latter nineteenth and early twentieth centuries.

As noted earlier, the following incidents mainly involve the north of Devon, and it should be remembered that until April 1877 the Exeter to Bideford line was of mixed broad (7' 0¼") and narrow (4' 8 ½") gauge track. I have attempted to deal with the incidents in the categories of 'on site / shunting type incidents', 'running line incidents', and 'miscellaneous and oddities' but some incidents will refuse to fit neatly into even these categories. Because of this, the chronology is necessarily rather erratic.

Construction of new railways often brought about accidents to the navvies working on them, and the Torrington Extension Railway from Bideford to Torrington was no exception. 1871 appears to have been a bad year, for three incidents were reported in the local press. On Friday 27th January *"a young man"* working on the new line was knocked over by a truck *"which passed over his leg in a slanting direction"*. He was rushed to North Devon Infirmary with a suspected fractured bone. On Wednesday 25th October, *"through inadvertency"* a navvy was caught between the buffers of some carriages and severely injured. Exactly one week later, an inquest was held into the death of William Dymond, a youth of about 16 years of age. On the Monday previous, the lad had been working in the Landcross tunnel apparently in charge of a horse and spoil waggon. *"As part of his duty, he left the horse attached to a muck waggon which he was leading from the 'turnout' to the mouth of the tunnel for the purpose of freeing the chain. The horse then darted off, and the waggon immediately knocked him down on the rails and passed over the lower portion of his body, crushing him in a fearful manner."* Despite constant medical attention, his injuries were so serious that he passed away at about three o'clock the following morning. A verdict of accidental death was recorded.

Shunting accidents were also unfortunately rather frequent and often resulted in fatal consequences but the victim of an incident in Bideford station in June 1863 was more fortunate. One John Bragg was engaged in unloading stone from a narrow gauge wagon in the station, when a broad gauge luggage train approached. At the same time some carriages were being moved along the narrow gauge track using a horse to pull them. The men in charge shouted a warning but it seems that Mr. Bragg was distracted by the engine of the approaching train and failed to hear them. The carriages struck the truck causing one of the stones to fall on to Mr. Bragg causing him serious injuries. *"He was conveyed home, and is progressing favourably, being able to walk out of doors."*

Less fortunate was John Davey, a young porter at Bideford who was assisting in the formation of the first train of the day on 26th August 1867. Whilst he was adjusting one of the coupling chains his foot slipped and became *"entangled under one of the wheels of the carriage near which he was standing."* Medical assistance was soon on the scene but the leg had to be amputated. Mr Davey was later said to be *"progressing favourably, but is in a very low state."*

As if to further underline the dangers of shunting, Thursday 3rd April 1873 was a black day in Devon. A breaksman named Belcher suffered a crushed leg at Morchard Road station on the North Devon Railway whilst assisting with shunting operations. On the same day a porter called Lock was

Opposite - Station Road / Church Hill, Ilfracombe, March 1951.

Under the canopy at Ilfracombe, March 1951.

killed in a similar incident near Okehampton.

A somewhat different incident was reported in the Gazette of 18th July 1882 when the paper reported that the daughter of the stationmaster suffered a fracture of the left arm. This was incurred *"while snatching a pet dog from the line in front of an approaching train. The young lady, in spite of what seems a narrow escape from a more serious mishap, maintained her complete self-possession."* One wonders what her father made of the episode!

Shunting accidents rear their head again in September of the same year, when John Parker, a railway porter, was injured at Holsworthy station. *"Whilst in the act of putting down the break so as to check the train in motion"* he had his foot run over by a wheel flange. Presumably he was attempting to slow some loose shunted wagons and got his foot on the line whilst wrestling with the brake lever. The doctor was soon on the scene and the injury transpired not to be as serious as first thought. Parker seems to have had an unlucky month, for it is reported that only a week before this accident he was returning home from Bude when *"he was thrown from his conveyance* (whatever that might have been) *when his head and face were sadly bruised and cut."* The article concludes, somewhat reassuringly, that *"the unfortunate young man is much respected by*

all who know him".

The dangers of the railway yard were not restricted to shunters. On 8th May 1863 an engine stoker was busy in the pit under his engine at Bideford engine shed. Being unable to reach certain parts, he called to his driver to move the engine slightly. *"The driver waited until the stoker had cried 'All right' and saying 'Look out then' moved the engine. Just at this point the stoker noticed a bucket which he thought was too near the wheel of the engine and he put out his hand to push it away. Regrettably he was not quick enough and the wheel ran over his hand crushing it fearfully."* He was rushed to Barnstaple Infirmary but the hand had to be amputated. The newspaper article reporting this incident closes with the grave salutation *"Men engaged in work which the least mistake makes so dangerous ought to insure in the Accidental office, when they would get a sum of money to help make up for their loss."* Sound advice indeed – one wonders if the reporter, or the paper, had an agency!

The benefit of insurance for railwaymen is also to be found extolled in the 'Southern Railway Magazine' and two incidents from this august publication are worthy of mention here. The first is somewhat out of the area under consideration, but still Southern Railway based, and relates to the death of a

RAILWAY ACCIDENTS AND RELATED INCIDENTS

signal linesman on 3rd August 1929 at Lyndhurst Road Station. Mr William Henry Gilham was struck by the 10.30 am Bournemouth to Guildford train and killed instantly. Mr Gilham subscribed to the 4d (insurance edition) of the Southern Railway Magazine and his widow received a cheque for £30 in regard to her claim. The magazine normally cost 2d, so the additional cost was a useful way of obtaining some form of insurance cover for railway staff.

A similar accident befell Sub-Ganger T. Osborn between Broad Clyst and Whimple in Devon on December 2nd 1928 but this was only reported in the Magazine after the previous case. Again the deceased subscribed to the 4d issue of the Magazine and his widow also received a cheque for £30. Whilst £30 does not seem a fortune in the twenty-first century, it probably represented quite a large sum at the time.

Tuesday 6th November 1888 was another black day for shunting accidents. The guard of the morning mail train, George Lovedon, was re-coupling the train to the engine after having detached wagons at Bideford. The driver asked a porter named John Wale to see why the guard was taking so long to couple up. Wale found that he had got caught between the buffers of the wagons and shouted to the engine driver, who pulled forward. It was however too late, for the unfortunate guard fell lifeless to the ground. The jury recorded a verdict of "accidental death" adding that there could be no blame attaching to anybody. *The jury expressed their sympathy with the widow and gave her their fees.* Mr Lovedon was a long serving employee of the railway and well known and respected in the area. The funeral took place the following Sunday afternoon and was exceptionally well attended, a special train being run from Exeter to allow the deceased's colleagues to pay their last respects. Such was the strength of feeling locally that the Gazette launched an appeal for the widow and children who were *"left totally unprovided for."* The offering from the Sunday morning service in the Parish Church which totalled £7. 14. 9d. was given to the bereaved.

This story had a rather chilling sequel almost exactly two years later, when on Monday 10th November 1890, the same porter John Wale was involved. Wale, then aged only 19, was engaged in coupling up the same train of the day when he was knocked by the wagon and fell, a wheel running over his leg. His injuries were at first thought to be minor, but the poor lad's condition worsened and two weeks later he was reported *"at the point of death."* Unfortunately I have been unable to find out whether or not he recovered but fear the worst.

A year earlier, tragedy stuck in the station yard at Holsworthy. On Saturday 20th April 1889, Bessie Coombe, aged about 12, the signalman's daughter, was sent by her mother to order some coal from the stores. She was seen standing by the coal stores as shunting was proceeding in the yard. The engine driver later *"felt something was wrong"*, and on stopping his engine he and one of the yard men were *"horror-stricken to see the corpse of Bessie Coombe."* She had clearly been hit by a wagon and the poor child had been crushed and decapitated.

Returning to the subject of the dangers of railway yards, the evening of Friday 4th May 1883 proved to be a terrible end to the week for Joseph Stanning, aged 33, of Helston. He was an employee of the Ordnance Survey Department and was returning home for the weekend. He had just alighted from the Holsworthy train at Okehampton and was crossing the line when *"he was struck by the engine of the Holsworthy branch, on leaving the turntable, knocked him down and almost severed his right leg just below the knee."* He was taken to the Devon and Exeter Hospital where he was suitably treated.

On a much more positive note it is interesting to read of the derailed truck on the 6.00 pm train from Exeter to Bideford on 6th November 1862. Somewhere between Instow and Bideford it was noticed, presumably by one of the footplate crew or the guard, that the last vehicle in the train was off the rails. The train was immediately brought to a safe halt but the crew was unable to re-rail the truck. The truck was detached and the rest of the train proceeded to Bideford where the station master summoned a group of his staff who then proceeded by special engine back to the scene. Fortunately this was the last train of the day along the line so time was not an issue. After a good deal of effort they managed to re-rail the truck by midnight and proceeded back to Bideford. All in all, a good night's work by all concerned.

On the evening of Friday 22nd May 1863, *"just as the last down train had left Fremington, the whistle of the engine sounded startlingly shrill, and, before the passengers had time to speculate on the cause, a tremendous shock was felt, accompanied with a smashing and grinding sound."* So began the report of the accident in which the train was wrongly routed into a siding instead of the main line. The locomotive hit the two trucks which were in the siding and smashed one against the retaining wall alongside. The locomotive suffered a broken buffer beam and several passengers were injured, although none very seriously. The driver was congratulated on stopping in short time and the blame was laid firmly at the door of the pointsman who had forgotten to change to points back after the trucks had been shunted into the siding. The paper again makes a comment in the form of a pertinent question; *"Do the Railway Company give wages enough to secure a proper class of men for these responsible posts?"*

20th October 1865 was the date of a 'mixed gauge' accident, near Pynes Bridge between Newton St. Cyres and Cowley Bridge on the North Devon Railway. The trains concerned were both 'up' trains: the narrow gauge mail train due into Exeter at 9.30 pm and a broad gauge goods train. The goods train is reported to have left Bideford only 15 minutes before the mail train. That the goods had got as far as Pynes Bridge is interesting. However, approaching Pynes Bridge the driver of the mail spotted the red tail light of the goods, shut off steam and applied his brakes. He was thus able to bring his speed down to about 10 miles per hour before his train hit the rear of the goods train, which one assumes was still moving at the time. The consequences were therefore nothing like as horrendous as they could have been. The engine and carriages of the mail remained on the tracks and there was little injury to the passengers or crew of the train. *"The injuries to the passengers*

Above - *Okehampton, looking east towards Coleford Junction and eventually Exeter.*
Opposite page - *Torrington, towards Bideford and from the approach.*

were not very important" stated the newspaper report! The guard's van and the next two trucks in the rear of the goods train were smashed and the guard suffered severe injuries to his skull. He was taken to the Devon & Exeter Hospital where, it is hoped, he recovered.

An incident on the narrow gauge Torrington & Marland Light Railway occurred on the afternoon of Saturday 9th June 1888. Two trains collided head on *"resulting in two or three men being seriously injured, while a great many others received bruises and cuts about different parts of the body. It appears that two engines were going in opposite directions – one towards the moor and the other returning with the men to Torrington. The driver of the one going to the works* (the moor - author) *ought to have stopped at Water Gate, so as to allow the other engine to pass on, but it seems that the driver either forgot to do so or did not know of this order. He went on and the engines ran into one another. The most seriously injured is a workman named Jackson."* Normally during the day, one engine worked from the works to the loop at the summit of the line near Yarde and another from Yarde to Torrington. Trains were exchanged here and thus only one engine occupied each section of the line. Presumably the Torrington bound train was taking the men home from their work and the other pulling empty wagons from the station. Exactly where the collision occurred is not clear, but it would seem that the normal work-

ing system was not in use on this occasion. Watergate was not normally used to pass as there was only a siding there and it was only a short distance out of Torrington.

A relatively rare occurrence happened on the evening of 29th June 1892 at Bideford station. The night mail train to London was of some length on this occasion and was due to depart at 7.52 pm. *"The signal was given to start, but lo and behold! the engine would not move. Neither forward nor backward would she go, and it quickly became evident that something was wrong."* Mr Dalby, the station master promptly wired Barnstaple for another engine which arrived in due course, but it was nearly an hour later before the mails were on their way. *"It transpired the next day that one of the valves of the engine was out of order."*

Runaways feature in 1897 when misfortune befell the 'up' early morning goods from Torrington. The train comprised engine, six loaded trucks of clay and two guard's vans. The train had just passed through Bideford station when the coupling in the centre of the train broke. The engine, van and three trucks continued down the incline and stopped at the goods station. The remaining three trucks and van then *"rushed down the incline at a terrific rate, and dashed into the other vans, smashing them completely up."* Fortunately no one was injured although two men *"jumped away just in time. The down mails had to be sent on to Torrington by foot, the line*

'The only way to travel'- a mixed working between Torrington and Halwill Junction.

being blocked by wreckage."

The next example involves a fairly straightforward running-line collision which occurred at Fremington. Located on the North Devon coast between Bideford and Barnstaple, Fremington station was the scene of another mixed gauge colli-

sion on 23rd September 1869 when the 3.10 pm 'up' mixed goods and passenger broad gauge train from Bideford to Crediton was hit by the 1.25 pm 'down' narrow gauge passenger train from Exeter to Bideford. The details of this incident have been well documented elsewhere but details of a subsequent court case add an interesting element of 'human interest' to the matter. Briefly, the details of the accident revolve round the fact that, although at the time Fremington was provided with a passing loop; it had only one platform, on the 'down' side. 'Up' trains wishing to use the platform had therefore to cross to the 'wrong' side. The 3.10pm had left Bideford 5 minutes late and arrived at Fremington at 3.33 pm, still 5 minutes late. It was directed into the platform road and, after passengers had alighted or joined the train, the pointsman directed the driver to run forward over the points at the Barnstaple end of the loop and set back into the 'up' side of the loop to allow the 1.25 pm from Exeter into the platform. This latter was due at Fremington at 3.35 pm. As the engine of the 'up' train was passing through the points at approximately 3.34 or 3.35 pm, the driver spotted the 'down' train heading towards him round the curve about 200 yards distant. The driver's prompt action in reversing was too late to avoid a collision and the engine was struck by that of the approaching 'down' passenger train. The leading and driving wheels of the broad gauge engine came off the track as did the leading brake van, but the rest of the train was unharmed. Only one passenger in the train complained of any injuries. We shall deal with her later! The narrow gauge train kept to the rails and only minor damage was sustained by the locomotive. The subsequent Board of Trade enquiry was conducted by Lt. Col. Hutchinson who held that the driver of the 'down' train had passed the distant signal at danger which was against the LSWR's single line regulations. Col. Hutchinson also blamed the pointsman for allowing the 'up' train to shunt when the 'down' train was due. He concluded that the accident would not have occurred if there had been a platform on the 'up' side of the loop and recommended that one be constructed *"and that 'up' and 'down' trains always use the proper lines of the loop at this and other stations of the North Devon line."*

The injured passenger in the broad gauge train, a Mrs Emily Sweet, took action against the LSWR to recover compensation for injuries and consequential losses on her own and her husband's behalf, estimated at £2,000 each! The case was heard at the Sheriff's Court in Exeter in August the following year before the Under Sheriff, Mr Justice James and a special jury. It appears that Mr Sweet was in business as a house decorator and had extended this to include furniture dealing. Mrs Sweet was in charge of this aspect of the business. The plaintiffs argued that the business was suffering as a result of Mrs Sweet's injuries and this involved Mr Sweet as well as his wife. The lengthy newspaper report of the trial tells of the testimony by many colleagues and acquaintances to support the case of Mrs Sweet's continuing after effects, which appeared to be somewhat difficult to quantify. A medical witness for the LSWR suggested that the symptoms were consistent with her age! A long spell of concussion appears to have been the general impression given. Whilst counsel for the LSWR agreed that liability had been admitted, he questioned the amount of the damages claimed and in the end the jury, after fifteen minutes deliberation, awarded Mrs Sweet £300 and her husband £225. Their counsel stated that his clients were *"perfectly satisfied with the verdict!"*

Fremington station features again in accident statistics

in 1870 when Porter Hammett was run over by wagons during a shunting operation sustaining injuries from which he later died. A verdict of accidental death was recorded at the inquest. As is well known, probably the most dangerous job on the railways was always that of shunter and these incidents clearly underline that fact.

The earliest newspaper report considered here reaches back to November 1857 and the article's heading ***"Fatal Accident – A Singular Dream"*** immediately attracted my attention. The story has such an element of the supernatural about it that I quote the newspaper article verbatim.

"On Wednesday last, a man named Thomas Mills met with his death whilst working on the new line of railway now in progress near Offwell, about two miles from Honiton. The circumstances connected with his death are very curious. It appears that on the previous night he dreamt he saw his youngest child run over by the train, and he awoke much frightened; eventually he slumbered off again, but the same thing entered his mind a second and third time. The following morning he related his dream to the people of the house he was lodging with, and afterwards proceeded on his way to work. He had not, however, been there very long before a waggon came dashing through the cutting in which Mills was engaged; there was not enough room for him to get out of the way; he was knocked down, and the wheels of the waggon passed over his body. Medical aid was promptly obtained; but the poor fellow expired in about two hours afterwards. Mills is a native of Torrington and has left a wife and seven children." No details are given of how the waggon came to be running away – for that is what seems to have happened. A very tragic tale with 'spooky' overtones which has echoes of Charles Dickens' story 'The Signalman'.

A serious accident occurred on Saturday 6th February 1881 near Dunsland Cross on the Holsworthy to Okehampton line. Sarah Smale, a passenger on the 5.05pm train to Okehampton got up to look out of the window when the door flew open. *"She held on for a second or two, but the door sprang back and threw her off. The stoker happened to see her fall. And the train was at once stopped and put back. The girl was found lying insensible, and in that condition was conveyed to her home in Dunsland Cross."* She apparently suffered a sprained ankle and was severely bruised on the head and shoulders. A very lucky young lady, it would appear.

Not so the lady involved in an ***"Appalling Fatality near Bideford"*** just over a year later, on Saturday 17th June 1882. The long article reporting the tragedy in the Gazette began *"One of the most deeply painful and terrible events that have ever taken place in Bideford occurred on Saturday morning."* Miss Jessie Tanton of Bideford was a well known person in the area and had a business in Torrington making card boxes. On the day in question, she took the morning mail train from Bideford to proceed to her factory. *"On arrival of the train at the station a hat and small basket, at once recognised as belonging to the lady named, was found in an empty compartment, but there were no traces of the lady herself."* Searches at both stations were at once instituted and three boatmen set off up the river, apparently of their own volition and seemingly fearing the worst. The boatmen returned before nine o'clock with the sad news that they had recovered the body of Miss Tanton in the river near to the railway bridge. They *"brought the body back to Bideford and delivered it at her mother's house in Marine Place."* It seemed that she had fallen from the train into the river and drowned. An inquest was immediately convened and was held the same evening before the Deputy Coroner and a Jury at the Commercial Hotel in Bideford. The body had been identified by a Mr C E Clemow, a friend of the deceased. Witnesses were called and testified as to the state of mind of the deceased prior to the accident. She had appeared as normal; perhaps in lower spirits than usual, but nothing which suggested anything untoward. Edgar Cox, Esq., surgeon, deposed that he was Miss Tanton's usual medical attendant and that he had not seen her professionally for many years. He reported on his examination of the body. *"There are only two or three very slight bruises; one on the front of the right elbow joint and a very slight injury on the right hip. The back of the left hand is smeared with what looks like black paint."* He was of the opinion that she had fallen out of the train and into the water and *"not struck with force against anything."* The next witness was Richard Brock a porter at Bideford station who stated that he had seen the deceased on board the train and that she was standing looking out of the window on the eastern, left hand, side of the carriage. He stated that the door was hasped but did not know if it was locked. *"It is not usual to lock the doors."* Another porter, Frank Hill confirmed that he had seen Miss Tanton get into the compartment and he had seen her seated before the train departed. He also stated that men were working on the bridge when he later walked up the line, but that they could not have been there when the train passed. Charles Heard, a passenger on the platform at Torrington noticed the hat and basket in the compartment when the train arrived. The door was apparently not properly shut. He was sure that no one came out of the compartment as he was standing opposite it. At this point the jury decided that they should inspect the scene and see the height of the parapet and *"the whole of the jury thereupon drove off for that purpose."* They noted that the floors of the railway carriages were higher than the top of the bridge parapet. When they had returned Richard Dunn, who was working on the bridge, gave evidence. He stated that he and three others were engaged in tarring the bridge and had walked up to it from Bideford. The mail train passed them at about half a mile before they reached the bridge at about five past six. They were on the left hand side of the track and did not see anyone looking out. They reached the bridge about ten or fifteen minutes later. They did not see anything untoward. Afterwards, when they had heard of the accident *"we saw what looked like foot marks on the bridge."* Dunn continued *"I saw small nail marks on the parapet. These marks were on the top. It was about 30 feet from the footmarks to the last traces of the marks on the parapet."* There were also some small pieces of material from Miss Tanton's coat on the parapet. The first man in the group, James Bennett, was ahead of his colleagues and stated that he saw a lady looking out of the window on the nearside as the train passed Mr Turner's lime-kiln. *"She was*

leaning with her breast against the door." He was of the opinion that the marks on the parapet were those of a woman's foot because they were so small, and there were marks of a "slur" following the foot-prints. There were some pieces of stuff of a grey colour entangled in the rivets on the top of the parapet. These matched the ulster coat worn by Miss Tanton. Mr Clemow stated that it was a habit of Miss Tanton's to keep her hands in her pocket, and also to take her hat off in the train, and more particularly to watch the fishing and to look out for the rising of fish. The Coroner summed up at length, noting that there was nothing to indicate that Miss Tanton had any intention of taking her own life and that it was well known that she had a habit of standing with her hand in her pocket looking out of the window. The Coroner noted the fact that when the body was discovered one hand was still in her coat pocket. He surmised that Miss Tanton might have caught her clothing in the door when she first entered the carriage and *"that after releasing herself she did not properly secure the door, or that from some cause the door might have given way whilst deceased was leaning against it."* He concluded by suggesting that the jury might well be fully justified in finding a verdict of accidental death. After less than fifteen minutes deliberation the jury duly returned with the verdict: *"That the said Jessie Susannah Tanton was drowned as a result of an accidental fall from a railway carriage while passing over the River Torridge on a journey from Bideford to Torrington."* The jury decided to give their fees to the Bideford Dispensary. It is interesting to note that the hearing which commenced at 5.30 pm did not conclude until a few minutes before midnight.

Chilling sequels return again when the perils of the yard were yet again illustrated on Saturday 24th March 1883 at Torrington. This time however, the unfortunate victim was Richard Dunn, the labourer on the bridge in the previous incident. This time he was working on the new turntable at Torrington station and had travelled from home in Bideford on the early 'down' mail train. He was apparently on his way across the tracks to warm up his tea for breakfast when he became aware of an approaching engine. Unfortunately he caught his foot and slipped, and the engine ran over the leg just above the foot. The leg had to be amputated and *"the sufferer is now going on as well as can be expected. No blame is attached to the engine driver, as he had blown his whistle at starting and did not observe Dunn."*

At the other end of the time scale we are considering is the case of the "***Railway Mystery at Barnstaple***" reported in the North Devon Weekly Gazette. The body of William Watts, aged 82, a retired farmer of Chittlehampton, was found by the line a short distance from Barnstaple Junction station on Thursday 6th October 1927. The body was found lying between the metals by a naval pensioner who was walking along the river bank. He stopped the next passing train and *"a stretcher was fetched"*. The driver of the previous 'down' train was advised of the incident when he reached Torrington, but knew nothing of the fatality. On examination of his locomotive he *"found evidence on the brake rod of the mishap"*. Watts' hat and overcoat were found hanging on the railings near the line and his

Seen from the Torrington Bay platform is this view of Halwill Junction. The train in the platform has arrived from the direction of Okehampton.

wallet contained letters to his two daughters. What these contained was not made public. It appeared that Watts was prone to bouts of depression although he had no financial worries. The inquest jury found that he *"was found dead on the line as a result of the train going over him"*, and added that there was no blame attaching to the engine driver.

The case against a boy for stealing tickets from Torrington station would appear to fit under the heading 'miscellaneous and oddities'. The case involved the disappearance of 35 tickets from the booking office at the station in September 1882. The defendant, a lad of tender years it is thought, had been seen on several occasions coming out of the station booking office and, when arrested had some money on him but no tickets. Circumstantial evidence seems to have ruled the day and the boy was found guilty and sentenced to six stokes of the birch rod!

A far more serious incident involving a boy was reported in the newspaper of 29th January 1884. The article is headed, rather interestingly *"**An attempt to throw a train off the London and South Western Railway.**"* Not it transpires a strong-arm act from the circus, but the placing on the line of various platelayers' tools and equipment. The case involved the 2.00pm train from Bideford on Sunday 27th January. Navvies had been working on the line on the previous day and had left their tools at the side of the track. As the train approached Instow, Thomas Poole the driver, noticed some obstruction on

the line and *"the distance being so short, he put on steam to clear it if possible, but found the obstruction too much; therefore he stopped the engine immediately."* He found three fishplates, four bolts and about 20 stones on the line, having already passed over some crowbars, pickaxes and shovels. The debris was cleared and the train proceeded on its way unharmed. One assumes that the train had been slowed to a crawl by the time the first obstructions were reached and that a full application of the brakes stopped the train within seconds. If the driver had not been so vigilant, a derailment could well have occurred. The boy pleaded guilty before the County Bench to placing the things on the line, but said others were involved as well. These other boys gave evidence but were successful in convincing the court that they had been minor players in the incident. The ringleader was much less fortunate. *"The Bench considered that an example should be made in the present case, for the sake of the protection of the public, and they sentenced defendant to six weeks imprisonment with hard labour and afterwards to be kept in a reformatory for three years."*

Even the waiting passenger is not immune from the perils of accident, or in this case, the negligence of others. Mr George Heard of the Royal Hotel was standing on the platform at Bideford talking with a friend when the Torrington train arrived. A passenger, eager to alight, opened his door and jumped out before the train had stopped. *"The open door*

Barnstaple Junction towards Torrington and Ilfracombe. The platform on the right is original, that on the left was added in 1874 and converted to an island in 1924.

struck Mr Heard in the back and he was knocked senseless on the platform. It was at first thought he was seriously injured; but he is now recovering, although he has sustained a very severe shock."

On a more humorous note, the Bideford Gazette of 12th August 1890 draws readers" attention to a *"lamp-post close to the corner of the up platform lying on the ground badly smashed."* Not apparently the result of *"some bank holiday frolic"* or of weary souls hanging on to it for support. *"The truth, however, is that one of the "busses going to the station ran playfully against the post, and bowled it over – wild horses shouldn't make us name that 'bus!"*

The light-hearted vein continues in September when the paper makes reference to an *"improvement"* being carried out at Bideford station. Two weeks previously the paper had apparently hazarded a guess that the *"improvement"* might be a cow-house!! The issue of 9th September comments *"It appears that we were not far out, for one day last week a cow walked up the inclined way and into the new house quite naturally. That cow evidently thought the place was put up for her convenience!"*

Later in the same month the Gazette reports the close escape of Dr. Jones of Torrington who was nearly killed by the 6.16 pm down train as he was crossing the line from the Royal Hotel Refreshment Room. He apparently stumbled and fell on the rails. *"Rising to his feet he managed to scramble to the platform just as the engine was upon him. Indeed, some say the buffer actually struck him. Dr. Jones, who looked pale and shaken* (I bet he did – author) *proceeded by train to Torrington."*

"Shocking" tragedy returned to Bideford on Tuesday 26th July 1904 when William Saunders, a 51 year old builder from Barnstaple was hit and killed by the 5.37 pm from Barnstaple as it was about three-quarters of a mile from Bideford station. It was raining heavily at the time and the engine driver saw a man step in front of the train as it approached. There was no time for the poor driver to do anything and he said that he *'felt the engine go over the body'.* Witnesses at the inquest gave evidence that Mr Saunders had shown no signs of suicide but a letter to his wife discovered in his wallet suggested his death could well have been intentional. The deceased was of poor sight and hearing, and had been *"run down"* in health for some time. (An unfortunate choice of phrase in the circumstances – author.) The Coroner instructed the jury to consider

RAILWAY ACCIDENTS AND RELATED INCIDENTS

the possibility of accident but they returned a verdict of *"suicide whilst temporarily insane."* As on a previous occasion, they expressed their sympathy with the family to whom they donated their fees.

Finally, to return to shunting incidents brings us to the exchange sidings at the Marland Clay Works on Friday 9th September 1932. The 6.25 am mixed train from Torrington to Petrockstow had stopped to collect some loaded wagons from the clay works sidings. The guard of the train, Frederick Rowland was acting as shunter and gave the signal for the driver of the train to back up to the wagons. Having started to move the train, the driver then saw Rowland's coupling pole in the four-foot. Looking back, the driver saw Rowland himself also lying in the four-foot. Apparently he had been releasing the brake on the first wagon when he had slipped and fallen under it and the locomotive had run over him. He was seriously injured and was taken to Torrington Cottage Hospital and then to Bideford Hospital where his leg was amputated. He was able to make a statement to the effect that the accident had been his own fault and not that of the driver. Unfortunately his injuries were so severe that he died a month later. Mr Rowland has a claim to fame in that, whilst he was working at Woking, he won the competition to find a name for the 11.00 am 'down' express from Waterloo to the West of England. That name of course was the "**Atlantic Coast Express**."

I hope that this brief dip into some of the accidents and incidents which prevailed in the earlier years of railways has been of interest, showing as it does not only some of the wide variety of incidents which arose, but also the dangers inherent in railway operation. The work of the accident investigators – the officers of the Board of Trade Railway Department - is only briefly touched upon in the recommendation by Lt. Col. Hutchinson after the Fremington accident. He and his colleagues made many such recommendations for improvements in railway safety over the years, and whilst the railway companies were slow to act on most of them, ultimately the high standards of present day railway systems owe much to this fine body of men. It is also interesting to see how public attitudes to many things have changed over the past hundred plus years. Sentencing for offences could be most severe as we have seen. Jurors received fees for sitting on Coroner's juries and were not only prepared to work until midnight, but then in the case of hardship, to donate their fees to the bereaved or to charity. The Gazette reporters were particularly good at accurate reporting and their style of prose brings the story to life.

My sincere thanks go to Pat Slade and her colleagues of the Bideford Community Archive for their every generous help and guidance in searching out this material.

Halwill Junction, 3 July 1905. A goods train divided in two as it approached the station and the rear portion crashed into the front section on the level crossing. Two railwaymen received injuries with several pigs being killed and 25 wagons were damaged.

Opposite, top - *Fartherford Viaduct which carries the railway over the valley and the East*
Okement River north of Okehampton. The train, hauled by an Adams 4-4-0, is headed towards the direction of Exeter.

Opposite, bottom - *Rural delight at Umberleigh, 29 August 1956. The BR vehicle bears the designation, W3593.*

This page *- The northern end of Bideford station, in the top view seen towards Instow and Barnstaple Junction: the former just over nine miles distant. In the lower view is the Royal Hotel, for many years affording a Refreshment facility to waiting passengers. The steps form the latter establishment may be seen leading down on to the platform. The view through the station is towards Torrington.*

NAMING THE 'WEST COUNTRY' CLASS
(- well some of them at least!)

"...it gives me great pleasure...." - one can almost hear the words likely to have been used at stations in Dorset, Somerset, Devon and Cornwall as various members of the 'West Country' class were officially named. Often it was at the appropriately names station, No. 21C116 'Bodmin' for example making what was probably the one and only visit of a 'Pacific' to Bodmin North for the occasion - no photographs unfortunately. *(I think it unlikely to suggest that Nos. 34028 or 34029 made similar one-off trips...... !)*

Invariably it was the great and the good who were invited to the dais, those on this page involved with No. 34031 'Torrington' on 24 November 1949. Speaking at the microphone is T E

Chrimes, Motive Power Superintendent of the Southern Region. Stood on the right of the photograph is, we are advised, the Mayor of Torrington, Alderman E A Holwill, with the Mayoress alongside.

A few weeks later, on 29 December 1949 at Weymouth, it was the turn of No. 34091. Speaking at the microphone is S B Warder, Mechanical & Electrical Engineer for the Southern Region, whilst the actual unveiling was performed by the Mayor of Weymouth and Melcombe Regis, Alderman J P Burt JP.

Also in November 1949, the 25th had seen No. 34092 'Wells' named at Priory Station. The engine had entered service from Brighton two months previously and was then based at Stewarts Lane. The naming was performed by the Mayor of Wells, Alderman E M Kippax. Also in the view opposite top, are on the left the Lord Bishop of Bath and Wells, The Rt. Rev. W Bradfield, and representing the Southern Region, A Earle Edwards, Southern Division Superintendent. Also present from BR, but out of camera, was R G Pole, Western Region Divisional Superintendent from Bristol.

Subsequent to the formalities and official photographs, it was the turn of the waiting masses to have the opportunity to visit the footplate, the assembled throng having a high proportion of females present. Notice how despite the occasion, the cleaners had been unable to reach either side of the centre-line of the casing.

On 14 April 1950, less than six months after the ceremony, the name was altered to 'City of Wells' - perhaps an attempt to indicate the importance of what is England's smallest cathedral city. Even so, no similar change was made to other members of the class also named after cathedral cities, Nos. 34001-3.

It was customary to invite the local VIPs to the footplate, most clearly relishing the occasions: as here at Wells with the Mayor and Bishop seen together with Mr Earle Edwards. So far as the Rt. Rev. is concerned, there appears to be a certain genuine enthusiasm from his expression - but perhaps that is no wonder, after all there was a man of the cloth who featured in a leading role in 'The Titfield Thunderbolt', filmed not far away in 1952.

THE SOUTHEN PNEUMATIC PULL-AND-PUSH SYSTEM

Martin Brakespear

Imagine a cold winter's night, about 6.00pm, Dorchester South (BR naming, it was just Dorchester in SR days), and a 12-year old school boy on the down platform: having stayed for the after school woodwork club to make up the framing for his Hornby railway base-board. He was awaiting the Weymouth train ex-Waterloo and Bournemouth, normally Bulleid pacific-hauled. Then to his surprise, 20 minutes before his own train was due, the flickering head-code lights could be seen of a train arriving from Bournemouth.

A further surprise when, as it pulled into the severely curved down platform, it was seen to be an 'M7' hauling two antique coaches. A quick enquiry of the driver, busy at the controls in the cab, elicited the reply that this service was not Weymouth bound, but was in fact returning to Bournemouth in a few minutes. This was interesting, because there were no longer any loco servicing facilities at Dorchester, the shed having shut over a year before, and the timing given did not seem to allow for running the engine around the train, let alone turning it. But then, without further ado, the driver collected up his bag and left the cab, moved to the rear of the train and entered the rear compartment. In the meantime, the engine seemed to be panting leisurely - from its exertions in pulling the two coaches from Bournemouth? (It might even have started from Swanage, reversing at Wareham, this being one of the many useful services that the Marples / Beeching destruction of the railways did away with.)

The fireman remained in the engine cab and busied himself making up the fire and putting water into the boiler. Shortly afterwards he looked out of the cab, and with a bell ringing, the train started off in the direction of Bournemouth, crossing over to the up line as it ran towards the new signal box

recently commissioned consequent upon the removal of the old LSWR elevated box at the London end of the down platform. The engine was still at what was now the back end of the train.

What I had just witnessed, sadly for the first and the last time, was Push-and-Pull working - Southern style. Shortly afterwards, such workings on BR disappeared.

As the industrial revolution took hold in Britain, it became necessary for workers to travel further and further to their place of work, a fact recognised by legislation forcing the railway companies to run workers' trains at extremely cheap fares. This same industrialisation of Britain led to the development of readily available cheap road transport, initially in the form of trams, and then increasingly into the mid 20th century, of bus and car transport. The railways thus found themselves in the quandary of having developed at great expense the need for local people transport, but seeing it taken away by cheaper forms of transport.

They needed to respond, and the Southern and its predecessors, the LSWR and LBSCR in particular, opted mainly for electrification; in fact the right solution. Other alternatives though were available. All of the railways tried various attempts to reduce operating costs on suburban lines whilst speeding up the service. One of these was the steam railmotor, where a bogie on a standard coach was replaced with a steam powered unit. Later still came alternative forms of power along similar lines, such as the relatively expensive diesel / petrol powered unit, which in time would become the norm.

But to return to earlier, steam days, and the generally preferred option was the push-pull idea. In this system, existing steam locomotives were modified and matched with adapted coaches so that it was possible to drive the whole train

Opposite page - Peasmarsh Junction, south of Guildford, the driver of a Horsham bound train is taking the single line staff for the section to Bramley and Wonersh. Set 753 was former LBSCR 'arc-roof' stock . Although no exact date is given, the view was taken at a time when this particular formation consisted of vehicle Nos. 6929 and 2191 and was allocated to Cranleigh for Guildford - Horsham workings. Details of the propelling engine were not recorded.
John Davenport / Transport Treasury

Right - 'M7' No. 30328, propels the 2.45 pm, Andover Junction to Southampton Terminus, via Eastleigh, service into Fullerton junction on 2 October 1958. Set No. 385 comprises corridor vehicles of former LSWR stock. This particular set was normally allocated to Bournemouth West as a relief set and was being used here for a substitute DEMU working.

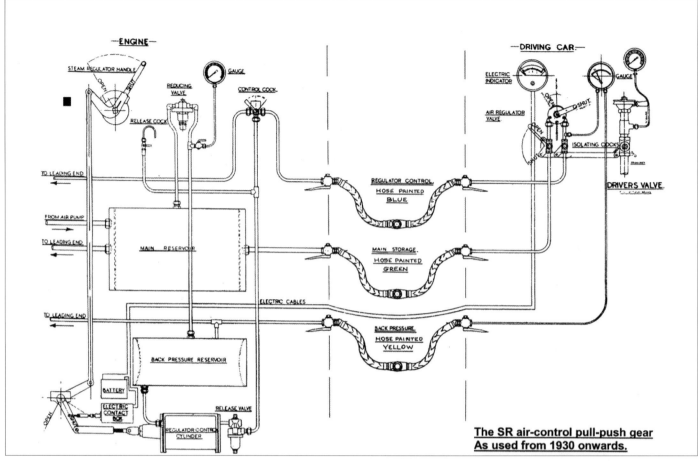

The SR air-control pull-push gear
As used from 1930 onwards.

in either direction without uncoupling the locomotive and running round. The savings were achieved by the reduction in labour costs, reduction in infrastructure costs, and potentially a faster service. (The Great Western adopted a similar, mechanical arrangement, referred to as 'auto-working'.)

THE SOUTHERN HIGH PRESSURE SYSTEM

Various ways of arranging control of the engine from the leading coach on the train were designed. The Southern Railway settled on a high-pressure pneumatic system from the 1930s onwards, employing a steam driven compressor, in the case of the 'M7s', mounted vertically on the smoke box. To understand how the system worked and what the engine crew had to do to ensure safe operation, we can analyse the mechanics of the equipment and then look at a sample of the rule book instructions for the crew.

A study of the diagram above shows the key function controlled by the driver in the leading coach is the regulator position. This controls the flow of steam from the boiler to the cylinders. All other footplate controls, the reverser for linking up, water injection into the boiler, whistle, cylinder drain cocks and sanders, were operated by the fireman remaining on the footplate and who responded to bell codes given by the driver in the driving trailer, or, in some cases, by his own (the Fireman's) knowledge of the road. From the left hand side, the steam-driven air pump is not shown, but the supply from it is

seen mid-diagram leading into the 'Main Reservoir'. The Reservoir is necessary because any sudden demand for air will deplete the pressure from the pump, and the reservoir buffers this so the pressure remains almost constant in the right hand side of the system.

Two pipes are seen coming out of the ends of the Reservoir. One under the 'from air pump' pipe is labelled 'to leading end', and the right-hand pipe goes to the controls in the 'Driving Car' via a connecting pipe labelled 'Main Storage' and coloured green through the coaches' air connections. (The pipe connectors between the coaches were colour coded and fitted with a high pressure connection different from the vacuum and steam heat systems to avoid incorrect attachments.) In fact, these two supply pipes are the same, one to each end of the locomotive. Notionally, a push / pull set could be air connected simultaneously to both ends of the locomotive as per the Great Western auto-train practice, but the Southern did not allow such working and it will be seen to be stopped by valves in the system later on. It did however allow the fitted coach set to be coupled to either end of the locomotive if required.

The main air supply is taken directly to the air regulator valve in the driving car. This in fact is the virtual (sorry for the computer jargon) steam regulator in the coach under the control of the driver. From the valve, a pipe leads back to the locomotive cab through a connection coloured blue to a 'Control Cock'. This is a two-way valve which switches the

Right - *The driver's compartment in an LBSC set. The Air Regulator (seen just above the seat) Valve handle is missing. The Train pipe valve is clearly visible, as is the vacuum and air pressure gauges (just) on the centre window pillar.*

Mike King collection

Bottom - *The drivers compartment in a push-pull set of former LBSCR stock. The left hand notice instructs drivers to give one beat on the bell - which must be acknowledged, before opening the regulator. The right hand notice is a reminder that passengers were not allowed in the compartment. Taken between Merstone Junction and Ventnor West, 7 August 1950.*

Dennis Callender

control air from the front to the back of the engine or *vice versa*, and it is this valve which prevents operative push-pull fitted coaches being coupled to both ends of the locomotive simultaneously. For operation from the Driving Cab, the valve must be set appropriately for that end. In both positions, the control air is directed down the pipe in the diagram to the 'release valve', and thence to the 'Regulator Control Cylinder'. The Release Valve functions as a separator for any water that is always present in compressed air, and which if allowed to build up, would eventually interfere with the correct operation of the valves and cylinders.

The driver can now operate the steam regulator remotely from the Driving Cab, and the sense of direction of the Air Regulator Valve mimics the steam regulator movement on the boiler. Looking at the diagram, if he moves the Air Regulator Valve clockwise, the piston in the Regulator Control Cylinder moves to the left and opens the Steam Regulator, and anti-clockwise he will shut off the air pressure moving the piston leftwards. Essentially, he can now drive the train from the Driving Car, with the fireman operating the other controls in the locomotive's cab. There is a problem however, in that compressed air is exactly that, compressible. The position of the piston in the Regulator Control Cylinder would always tend to move to full regulator opening without some constraint. In addition, removing the pressure from the Air Regulator Valve will not drive the piston back to the left hand side of the cylinder, and hence close the Steam Regulator. This constraint / back action is provided by introducing a balancing back pressure on to the back of the Cylinder piston.

If we go back to the Main Reservoir, we see a pipe going from the top of the tank to a 'Reducing Valve'. This valve automatically reduces the air pressure on the down side of the valve to a set pressure. It is a one-way valve and also prevents low pressure air leaking back into the rest of the system if the air falls below the low pressure for any reason. This reduced pressure air is stored in another reservoir, the 'Back Pressure Reservoir'. A pipe leading to a pressure gauge is seen leading off just below the Re-

An M7 with the air pump on the smokebox, and the air Back Pressure Reservoir on the tank top with associated pipework. The main Air reservoir on the 'M7's was under the front buffer beam and much larger. Notice the fireman taking the opportunity to catch up with his 'Daily Mirror'. No. 30048, Seaton Junction, 8 September 1960.

A E West

ducing Valve, and would be set to a predetermined pressure by the fitters on shed adjusting the Reducing Valve, although the locomotive crew could also adjust it if required. This back pressure air provides control of the piston in the Regulator Control Cylinder, acting effectively as a return spring. A key safety feature of this set-up, is that in the event of the air compressor failing, or a leak too big for the compressor to handle, there is always enough air stored and trapped in the Back Pressure Reservoir to shut the Steam Regulator Valve automatically. To shut the Steam Regulator, the driver has to shut the Air Control Valve and the back pressure pushes the piston in the Regulator Control Cylinder back to the shut position.

A gauge now uses a combination of the two system pressures to provide the driver with an indication of the Steam Regulator Opening. If we look to the right of the Air Regulator Valve on the diagram, we see an air pressure gauge connected to both the control pressure pipe coming out of the Air Regulator Valve, and to the Back Pressure Reservoir via a locomotive / coach connection coloured yellow. The dual gauge gives an indication of the balance of the two pressures acting on the Regulator Control Cylinder, and shows the driver that the system pressures are acting correctly. When the Air Regulator Valve is shut, the only reading is that if the back pressure, and when it is open, he will see that the main system pressure is greater than the back pressure air, thus moving the Control Cylinder piston. When balanced, the piston is stationary.

A number of other features essential for safety and communication between the driver and the fireman can now be explained.

The driver needs to know that the system is operable, and that it is responding to his remote actions in the cab. Looking at the bottom left hand corner of the diagram, we see a 'Battery' and an 'Electric Contact Box'. This is connected firmly to the crank arm in the Steam Regulator linkage, and moves proportionately with any movement of the Regulator. Electric wiring via plug-in connections is run from this to the Driving Car, where it is connected to an 'Electric Indicator'. When the linkage operates, the arm in the Contact Box moves over a series of resistances, and gives a variable voltage output according to its position. This is read by the Electric Indicator in the Driving Car, which is simply a volt meter labelled so as to give the actual opening of the Steam Regulator. The driver now has a clear indication of the Steam Regulator opening, and is re-assured that it is responding correctly to his action in the Driving Car.

On the diagram two interlinked valves (labelled 'isolating cocks'), are seen in the Main Storage pipe and the Regulator Control pipe. These must be open for the driver to operate from the Driving Cab. For safety, when the train is being driven from the locomotive, the driver must shut both of these valves, which happens simultaneously as they are linked. To do this, he removes the Air Regulator Control Valve handle, and secures the valve shut with a safety pin. He then uses the same handle to close the isolating cocks. The operation of the steam regulator in the locomotive cab cannot now be interfered with from the Driving Car.

If we follow the linkage from the Isolating Cocks to the right hand side of the diagram, there is a further linked valve labelled 'Drivers Valve'. This is the vacuum brake valve, and controls the vacuum in the train pipe and through the linkage, is always open when the control air valves are open. Above the linked shutoff valve, is the drivers brake handle, with a vacuum gauge attached to the pipe so that he can see how much brake he is applying. One of the safety checks he

Drivers compartment of a push-pull set working a special at Brighton Kemp Town, 5 October 1952.

Philip J Kelley

would do on moving to the Driving Car end, would be to see that this valve operated the brake vacuum, thus proving the vacuum system is both vacuum tight and controllable from the Driving Car. Again, on leaving the Car, the valve is automatically shut off, thus preventing interference with the braking system when the train is being driven from the locomotive footplate.

A final key safety element is the 'Release Cock' below and to the left of the Steam Regulator in the diagram. Should an emergency arise, the fireman could shut the regulator by opening this valve, so releasing the main control pressure. On doing so, the Control Cylinder back pressure would automatically shut the Steam Regulator. With the pressure released, the fireman would also be able to shut the regulator manually if all else failed.

As a means of communication between the crew when 'pushing', an electric bell was provided and bell codes were used to tell the fireman what actions the driver wanted him to take, such as moving the reverser, blowing the whistle, etc. The rules, garnered from the training booklet 'Practical Hints for Footplate Men' issued by the Southern, clearly state that the bell must be rung before the driver opens and shuts the regulator, and that the fireman must acknowledge before he does so. The only exception to this rule is in the case of emergency,.

Responsibility for coupling and uncoupling the Regulator control gears was the drivers, and he was aided in this by colour coding of the connecting hoses. These were:

1: Main Storage (green)
2: Regulator Control (blue)
3: Back Pressure (yellow)
4: Three-pin electric coupling
5: Earth wire

Any defects in the system, such as excessive back pressure (faulty or mis-set Reducing Valve), the bell not working, had to be reported immediately, and the engine run round the train so that it was always leading. However, compressed-air systems are not always the most reliable, and the conditions under which these locomotive systems must have operated along with poor working conditions on shed for the maintenance staff will have led to many defects. It was enlightening to read in Issue 3 of *The Southern Way* that Hugh Abbinnett had at least one occasion when the rules were broken and the fireman operated the Regulator from the locomotive cab under bell codes from the driver at the other end of the train. Sticking pumps, leaking cylinders, wrongly set reducing valves would all have driven conscientious crews striving to keep time to break the rules, but no doubt with full confidence that as a team they could manage the situation safely.

Some interesting information is missing. The usual operating pressure of industrial systems is 10 bar (150psi or thereabouts), and this would have been a manageable pressure for this system. But does anybody know what it actually was? Similarly, what was the back pressure? Although the system diagram clearly shows that having the locomotive sandwiched between two operative coach sets is not allowed, referring to Mike King's book *An Illustrated History of Pull-Push Stock (OPC),* there is a picture of the Swanage train with a LWSR push-pull set leading and Mk1's trailing off the Royal Wessex. The Mk1s were definitely not fitted stock, so it was only possible to drive from the LSWR stock end of the train. This either / or valve arrangement was a safety feature to prevent conflicting simultaneous control from both ends of the train. Referring again to the Swanage arrangement, operationally there was not a problem with returning the Wessex stock to Wareham this way, it saved an extra train working and it was perfectly safe re

Ventnor West with 'Terrier' No. 11 together with two former LCDR 4-wheel vehicles comprising either set 483 or 484, sometime between August 1924 and October 1928 when the name 'Newport' was allocated.

-marshalled behind the locomotive, but of course, the advantages of push-pull on arrival at Wareham were then muted, with some shunting and running-round being necessary.

Mike King's book lists the bell codes, and gives a fascinating insight to the revenue operations of these trains. Well worth a read.

Finally, a snippet from the past. My ex father-in-law was a craft apprentice at the Whitehead torpedo works at Ferry-bridge on the Portland branch. He regularly caught the push-pull train from Littlefields Halt near Weymouth, '02' hauled, locomotive leading to Portland, to travel to work with his fellow apprentices. Someone, and being a joker it was probably him, but he would not admit it, had a 'Thunderer' whistle - the same as the guards used. One particular guard would also habitually enter into intimate discussions at Rodwell with a lady who alighted there, and it seemed that the loco crew was a bit fed up with the hold up here every day. It was a situation easily discerned by young scallywag apprentices. On the day in ques-

tion, and as soon as the guard was busy talking to the lady, someone blew this private whistle. The loco crew, probably quite bored by now, started the train without looking back for the green flag - just as the apprentices expected they would: leaving the guard also out of sight on the steeply ramped footpath up to street-level. Apparently, by the time he realised, the train was out of the station and well on the way to Sandsfoot Halt, where it remained until he came puffing up red faced, hot and bothered and well out of sorts with the loco crew. The ensuing altercation from the 'four-foot' merely added to the joy of the apprentices, and also gave a good excuse for being late clocking in that day. Not surprisingly, the intimate discussions with the lady became much shortened for some time after that

Sadly, the Portland Branch has long gone the way of the Push-Pull idea. But hang on a moment, what's that lot on the West and East Coast main lines about? Some ideas are too good to lose after all.

Above - Push-pull fitted 'M7', No. 30053 on the turntable at Guildford shed. The main reservoir is seen under the front framing with the various connections labelled on the buffer beam. On the left of the smokebox is the pump.　　　*P F Winding*

Opposite page - The connections on the trailer coach end. As we look at the photograph, the two pipes left and one right below the head stock are the air control pipes. The third from left is the steam heat connection, and the one above the head stock is the train vacuum pipe for the brakes. The electrical connections can be seen hanging down between the two right hand pipes and next to the right hand buffer. This is S1050S recorded at Exeter central on 20 July 1960 at which time it carried red livery with black ends.

A E West

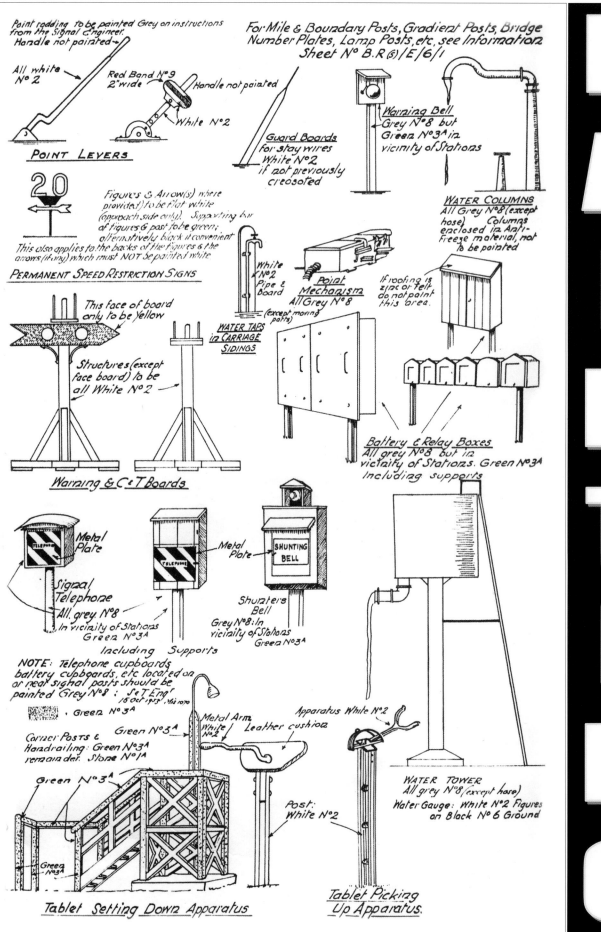

Paint rodding to be painted Grey on instructions from the Signal Engineer. Handle not painted

All white No 2

Red Band No 9 2" wide

Handle not painted

White No 2

POINT LEVERS

For Mile & Boundary Posts, Gradient Posts, Bridge Number Plates, Lamp Posts, etc, see Information Sheet No B.R.(S)/E/6/1

Warning Bell Grey No 8 but Green No 3A in vicinity of Stations

WATER COLUMNS
All Grey No 8 (except hose) Columns enclosed in Anti-Freeze material, not to be painted

Guard Boards for stay wires White No 2 if not previously creosoted

Figures & Arrow(s) where provided) to be Flat white (approach side only). Supporting bar of figures & post to be green; alternatively black it convenient

This also applies to the backs of the figures & the arrows (if any) which must NOT be painted white

PERMANENT SPEED RESTRICTION SIGNS

White No 2 Pipe & Board

WATER TAPS in CARRIAGE SIDINGS

Point Mechanism All Grey No 8

(except moving parts)

If roofing is zinc or felt do not paint this area.

This face of board only to be Yellow

Structures (except face board) to be all White No 2

Warning & C & T Boards

Battery & Relay Boxes All grey No 8 but in vicinity of Stations Green No 3A Including supports

Metal Plate

Signal Telephone
All grey No 8 In vicinity of Stations Green No 3A Including Supports

Metal Plate

TELEPHONE

SHUNTING BELL

Shunters Bell
Grey No 8: In vicinity of Stations Green No 3A

NOTE: Telephone cupboards, battery cupboards, etc located on or near signal posts should be painted Grey No 8 : S & T Eng' 15 Oct 1958 via roro

▨ . Green No 3A

Corner Posts & Handrailing: Green No 3A remainder. Stone No 1A

Green No 3A

Green No 3A

Metal Arm White No 2

Leather cushion

Apparatus White No 2

Green No 3A

WATER TOWER
All grey No 8 (except hose)
Water Gauge: White No 2 Figures on Black No 6 Ground

Post: White No 2

Tablet Setting Down Apparatus

Tablet Picking Up Apparatus.

PAINTING

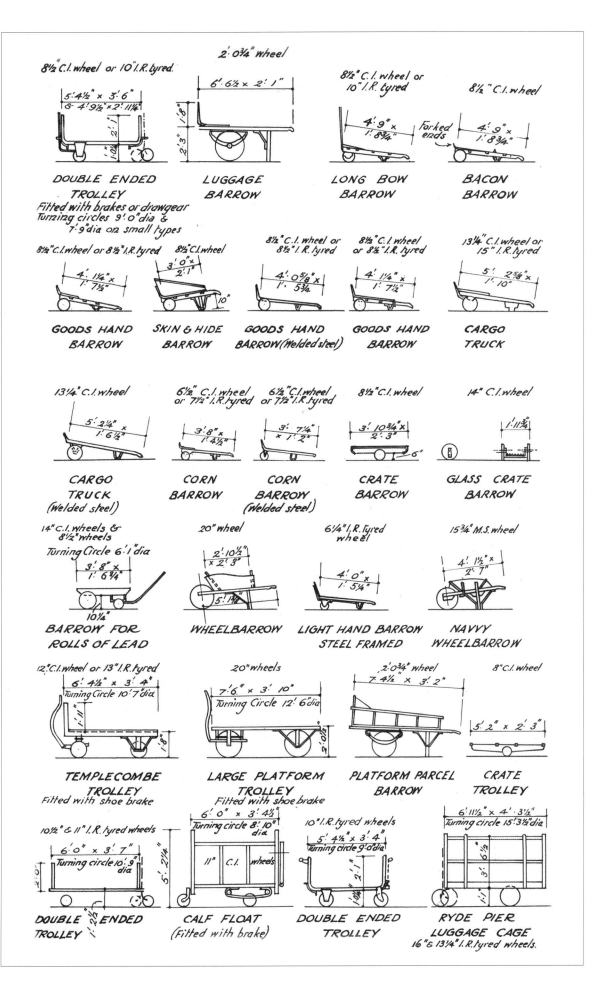

Left - SR painting styles for miscellaneous and lineside items from 1949, and re-confirmed in 1960.

Right - Barrow types and styles in use on the Southern Region in the 1950s.

8½" C.I. wheel or 10" I.R. tyred.

5' 4½" x 3' 6"
3' 4' 9½" x 2' 11¾"

DOUBLE ENDED TROLLEY
Fitted with brakes or drawgear
Turning circles 9' 0" dia &
7' 9" dia on small types

2' 0¾" wheel

6' 6½" x 2' 1"

LUGGAGE BARROW

8½" C.I. wheel or 10" I.R. tyred

4' 9" x 1' 8¾"

LONG BOW BARROW

8½" C.I. wheel

Forked ends

4' 9" x 1' 8¾"

BACON BARROW

8½" C.I. wheel or 8½" I.R. tyred

4' 1¼" x 1' 7½"

GOODS HAND BARROW

8½" C.I. wheel

3' 0" x 2' 1"

10"

SKIN & HIDE BARROW

8½" C.I. wheel or 8½" I.R. tyred

4' 0⅝" x 1' 5¾"

GOODS HAND BARROW(Welded steel)

8½" C.I. wheel or 8½" I.R. tyred

4' 1¼" x 1' 7½"

GOODS HAND BARROW

13¼" C.I. wheel or 15" I.R. tyred

5' 2⅝" x 1' 10"

CARGO TRUCK

13¼" C.I. wheel

5' 2¼" x 1' 6½"

CARGO TRUCK (Welded steel)

6½" C.I. wheel or 7½" I.R. tyred

3' 8" x 1' 4½"

CORN BARROW

6½" C.I. wheel or 7½" I.R. tyred

3' 7¼" x 1' 2"

CORN BARROW (Welded steel)

8½" C.I. wheel

3' 10¾" x 2' 3"

6"

CRATE BARROW

14" C.I. wheel

1' 11¾"

GLASS CRATE BARROW

14" C.I. wheels & 8½" wheels
Turning Circle 6' 1 dia

3' 8" x 1' 6¾"

10¼"

BARROW FOR ROLLS OF LEAD

20" wheel

2' 10½" x 2' 3"

5' 1¼"

WHEELBARROW

6¼" I.R. tyred wheel

4' 0" x 1' 5¼"

LIGHT HAND BARROW STEEL FRAMED

15¾" M.S. wheel

4' 1½" x 2' 7"

NAVVY WHEELBARROW

12" C.I. wheel or 13" I.R. tyred

6' 4½" x 3' 4"
Turning Circle 10' 7 dia

1' 11"

1' 8"

TEMPLECOMBE TROLLEY
Fitted with shoe brake

20" wheels

7' 6" x 3' 10"
Turning Circle 12' 6 dia

2' 0½"

LARGE PLATFORM TROLLEY
Fitted with shoe brake

2' 0¾" wheel

7' 4½" x 3' 2"

PLATFORM PARCEL BARROW

8" C.I. wheel

5' 2" x 2' 3"

CRATE TROLLEY

10½" & 11" I.R. tyred wheels

6' 0" x 3' 7"
Turning circle 10' 9 dia

2' 0"

1' 2½"

DOUBLE ENDED TROLLEY

6' 0" x 3' 4½"
Turning circle 8' 10 dia

11" C.I. wheels

5' 2¼"

CALF FLOAT (Fitted with brake)

10" I.R. tyred wheels

5' 4½" x 3' 4"
Turning circle 9' 0 dia

1' 10" 2' 1"

DOUBLE ENDED TROLLEY

6' 11½" x 4' 3½"
Turning circle 15' 3½ dia

6½"

3'

RYDE PIER LUGGAGE CAGE
16" & 13¼" I.R. tyred wheels.

Above, top line - From the 'South Western Gazette', two views of the training frame complete with both 'lock and block' and tablet instruments: also the embryonic model railway with single push along wagon. From the limited frame, it is difficult to see how the contemporary comment, "Other reported uses involved staff from the office of the Superintendent of the Line attempting to find solutions to operational problems", reproduced on page 38, might apply.

Above, main view - Numbered examples of some of the 93 items on display at the time of the IRS inspection visit.

Opposite page - Night class at Clapham from the collection of Ivan Jenkins. He records he attended the school on the following Tuesday evenings in 1947: 7 and 14 October, 4 and 18 November, and 2 December. (Keystone)

SIGNALLING SCHOOLS

Of the various articles that have appeared in 'Southern Way', one in particular which has created much interest is that reference the Clapham Junction Signal School (- Issue 7, July 2009). As mentioned in the accompanying text at the time, just as that particular issue was being made ready for printing, so additional information, reference the LSWR instructional facilities, arrived from Nick Pomfret. It was anticipated this alone would form the basis of a short follow up, although with several further items now to hand it seemed to make sense to wait until everything was available for what it is hoped will be a rather more comprehensive record.

The first reference to a signalling school appears in an undated issue, (possibly 1921), of the *South Western Gazette*. In this year there is reference to an IRS visit to the LSWR Signal Works at Wimbledon. From contemporary illustrations, it appears that whilst there was a considerable amount of material on view, this seemed to have related more to the technicalities of the equipment rather than the operation thereof. It was of course entirely possible that what were reported as 93 different items on view were deliberately assigned in consequence of the technical nature of the visitors. One particular reference may be

of slight amusement today and related to what is now the accepted reliability of electro-mechanical equipment but which was then still much of a novelty. "It would be difficult to single out any one exhibit where all were of importance, but the working of the electric point movement to be used at Feltham Gravitation Yard, connected to the hump boxes, was a surprise for most of the visitors, as it could be operated backwards and forwards 20 times in 15 seconds. Several trials were made to put the movement and apparatus out of order, without success." The same visit was also reported in the *Railway Magazine* in what was almost identical fashion.

In a separate issue of the *Railway Magazine* for the same year was a report of the school itself. Whilst answering many questions, it naturally throws up others, not least of which follows the very first line of what was a two page article, "Signalling Schools are now a feature of the training systems of all railway….". So, as far the area covered by *Southern Way*, where do the SECR and LBSCR fit in and also when was the Wimbledon installation established? The article goes on the report that the LSWR differed, "..from most of the others…" as it contained actual examples of the equipment referred to in the

lectures given, rather than these being seen in purely illustrative state. The equipment was also 'unboxed', so students might watch, and thus appreciate, the operations taking place. It was admitted this feature was aimed more towards those in the technical branch. The signalling equipment was arranged in a training block over two floors, and housed a lever frame, tablet instruments, telephones, 'Sykes - lock and block', other instruments, bells, plungers, repeaters, treadles, track-circuit control and electrically operated signals. Separate from the above was a set of three-wire Preece's block instruments.

Apart from training, the Signalling School was also charged with the evaluation of new equipment and familiarising the staff who would use it. At the time the article was penned, it was mentioned that two intermediate gate bell-indicators were under test before being sent to Cadhay and Gosford. Other reported uses involved staff from the office of the Superintendent of the Line attempting to find solutions to operational problems. The keenness of the students was also reported, "...some men prepared to stay in the signal box as late as 9.00pm."

The LSWR Signal Engineer, W J Thorrowgood[1], was said to have taken a considerable interest in the scheme,

and although it cannot be confirmed that he was the actual instigator, it would appear this was perhaps most likely.

At some stage the school moved from Wimbledon to nearby Clapham Junction, possibly in consequence of having out-grown the site, allied to the need to train more men. Certainly it was extant at Clapham in late 1947, as witness the accompanying correspondence from Ivan Jenkins of Seaford.

"I was present during the period 7 October to 21 December 1947. My attendance, as recorded in my 1947 diary, was on alternate Tuesday evenings: because at that time I was doing shift work as a booking-clerk at Worthing Central (North Office) - I would alternate between early and late turns, which meant I could not attend every week.

"These 'night classes' were provided free to any members of staff who had an interest in train operating. An entry in my diary in September notes, 'Have fixed up to go to Clapham Training School', which suggests that my attendance was arranged by the Station Master at Worthing. These were also the last classes run by the Southern Railway before nationalisation. Consequently the certificate I received later was from 'British Railways / Southern Region, Training School: Clapham Junction / Examinations 1948 / This is to certify that Mr. I G Jenkins has passed an examination in Double Line Block Working and Single Line Working'. The name John Elliot is typed above the words 'Chief Regional Officer'. Prior to being sent to Worthing Central in February 1947, I attended the Clerical Training School, also at Clapham Junction, starting in November 1946. The entrance to this school was on the south side of the footbridge and, I believe, you went through that room to get to the Signalling School. The Instructor at the Clerical School was Mr Farenden, and my recollection is that he was also the instructor of the Signalling School, so I believe it is he who appears in both of the photos. Of interest is that the model signals in your photo (Southern Way - Issue 7) go 'up' to indicate 'proceed' whereas the one in my photo is 'down' to 'proceed'. So sometime after 1947 resignalling even took place on the small railway."

Further recollections come from M G Harvey of Three Bridges [2].

"I was delighted to see in SW No. 7 three photos of the Southern's signalling school at Clapham Junction, which I attended, with seven or eight others, in the early part of 1962. The school was situated in the former footbridge, which had once given access to the inner platform footbridge. Entry was from this footbridge, via a passageway at the rear of an advertising hoarding. For a stranger it was not easy to find, and I do not remember any signs to indicate its presence.

"On entering the school, the budding signalman had to pass through three or four classrooms used by the clerical training school, before reaching the last and longest room at the very end. As can be seen in the first photo (SW7), the end of the building curved to the right: this was over the main through lines into Waterloo. Behind the camera was the instructors desk and blackboard, while to the left, sitting with our backs to the windows, were the trainees desks. The floor in the area of the desks at least, was covered in typical brown railway lino, else-

---

D. 671.

London, Brighton & South Coast Railway.

£10 REWARD.

WHEREAS, at about Two o'clock on the afternoon of Thursday, the 12th January, 1888, some evil-disposed person or persons did wilfully and maliciously tamper with the Norwood Spur Junction Distant Signal, by placing a large stone under the lever, so as to prevent its working, thereby seriously endangering the safety of the traffic,

The Directors hereby give notice that the above Reward of Ten Pounds will be paid to anyone who shall give such information as will lead to the conviction of the offender or offenders.

(By Order) **A. SARLE,**

LONDON BRIDGE TERMINUS, January, 1888.
Secretary & General Manager.

(1,000) Waterlow and Sons Limited, Printers, London Wall, London.

where there were bare boards with varying sized gaps between. Through these would drift smoke from passing trains, sometimes creating a minor fog at one end. Most of the time we were doing written work and only got to operate the model railway on a few occasions. Interestingly, I believe the local S & T staff were responsible for its maintenance. To the rear was an assortment of single line equipment and double line instruments, which could be used to signal trains on the model railway. At the far end were some full size signals and a motor worked point.

"The model was like a real railway in miniature, there was nothing toy about it. It was pure 1930s' Southern, down to the train liveries, signals, and the fully interlocked lever frame at the main junction in the Westinghouse style. Rolling stock comprised of two 'Portsmouth' motor coaches, two 'I3' tank engines - but with outside cylinders, two bogie coaches and a few goods wagons, all in pre-war SR colours. On the right on page 31 (SW7), is the stock storage box, this was also the first block post, with a section to the main junction of two pairs of double tracks. From here a normal double track layout led to the third block post where they became single for the final section to a single platform terminus with run-round loop. I believe the school had moved elsewhere before the fire, but I have no idea what became of the

railway. What a shame if it was broken up or sold off piecemeal. Our instructor thought it had come from Bassett Lowke."

To conclude this piece, we were delighted to receive some further notes from Alan Blackburn, "Several Pre-Group railways had Signal Schools equipped with signalled model railways. The one at Clapham was originally installed in the LB&SCR Signal School, which was located in a purpose built building in the goods yard at East Croydon. Clapham Junction was later considered to be a more convenient location and the East Croydon railway was moved following the closure of the former passenger overbridge linking West Hill with the station. (The bridge had already replaced the South Western Railway's cab road when today's platforms 7 and 8 were built.) Besides the Signal School, the bridge also provided accommodation for a Clerical Staff Training School.

"The railway was, I think, built to the old 'Gauge 3', with a track gauge of 2½ ins. There were two LB&SCR type 4-4-2 tank engines, a couple of carriages and a few wagons. (I never saw the 'Portsmouth' electric unit when I attended the school in 1957.) Otherwise the photographs show the railway very much as I remember it, except the Tyers (?) signal frame shown had been replaced by a new one built by the Hayward Signal Company. This firm had a small factory on the country

Collection, Ivan Jenkins. (Keystone)

side of Coulsden South station. The only other Hayward Signal Co. signal frame I ever came across was a 16 lever frame in Oakhanger 'block-post' on the Longmoor Military Railway.[3] Longmoor of course had a very fine Signal School railways, theirs was to 'O' gauge, supplied by Bassett Lowke. The big difference between the two being that the at Longmoor it worked very well, whereas the Clapham one sadly did not. It was probably only dirty but although the Clapham Signal & Telegraph people were supposed to maintain it, they were never seen.

"Harry Dallery was the instructor in 1957, a former Relief Signalman who had to come out of Box work due to ill health. The course only lasted two weeks and was entirely theoretical, based on learning the relevant Rules & Regulations, following which you went to the box you had been appointed to for practical instructions by the men already there. Usually you were 'passed-out' by the Area Inspector after a further two or three weeks. As most new signalmen were previously signal lads used to large mainline boxes and who thus already knew their Rules and Regs., it all worked very smoothly.

"I do not know when the school closed, but I seem to remember there was a fire on the bridge in the early sixties and afterwards the bridge was demolished. I think the school was then relocated to Beckenham but I doubt the model railway went there as a friend purchased a model signal that had been in the signal school at a Model Railway Club Exhibition in the Westminster Central Hall and this was not long after the fire."

1- Thorrowgood, W.J. - Joined the LSWR at Guildford in July 1877, as a junior clerk, moved to Godalming in the same year and shortly afterwards was transferred to Wimbledon, then in July 1879 to the Telegraph Office at Waterloo. In July 1899 became Clerk-in-Charge, but in 1903 after four years in this position, was appointed Chief Technical Assistant in the Telegraph Department. In 1907, on the retirement of J.P. Annett, the Telegraph and Signal Departments of the LSWR were amalgamated and Thorrowgood was appointed General Assistant for Signals and Telegraphs. He succeeded A.H. Johnson as Chief although then in an acting capacity in December 1918. The substantive appointment was confirmed from 1 January 1920. Appointed Signal and Telegraph Superintendent of the Southern Railway in 1923 and subsequently retired in September 1927. Died, 18 October 1928, aged 66 years. He was a member of the Institution of Electrical Engineers; the Institute of Transport; the Institution of Railway Signal Engineers (President for the year 1924, after being a Member of Council for many years); and a member of the Signal Section of the American Railway Association. He served as chairman of the Railway Clearing House Signal Engineers' Conference, and of the Railway Clearing House Telegraph Engineers' Conference. He was also a Fellow of the Permanent Way Institution, an Hon. Member of the Institution of Locomotive Engineers (see Paper No. 197: Signalling from a driver's point of view. *J. Instn Loco. Engrs.*, 1926, 16, 463-85. Disc.: 485-97), a Fellow of the Royal Astronomical Society, a member of the British Astronomical Association, and a Fellow of the Royal Society of Arts. In connection with standardisation he served on the Railway Standard Committee, also on several British Engineering Standards Association Committees. He was a member of the Ministry of Transport Committee on Light Signals. During his tenure of office he was responsible for the installation of many improvements of the greatest importance in connection with telephones, signalling, especially his pursuit of colour light signalling on the Southern Railway

Papers: (Institution of Railway Signalling Engineers via Nock).
The maximum regulating resistance and maximum shunt resistance of track circuits. (April, 1918).
Renovation of Leclanche porous pots and the re-use of the interiors of spent dry cells. (April, 1919).
Magnetic storms (April, 1921).
Some problems of automatic train control (July, 1921).
Automatic telephone switchboards, Waterloo, Eastleigh and Southampton . (October, 1923).
Four aspect colour light signals. (March, 1926).
Four aspect colour light signals and power signalling in practice. (May, 1927).
2 - Having successfully passed all the exams, Mr Harvey duly became a signalman at Dorking Town. His recollections of this, as well as his later career as a signalman at Three Bridges and Redhill will feature as an article in the 'Southern Way' Issue 12, (October 2010).
3 - See http://www.eastcoulsden.co.uk/news11.html for more information on the firm of Thomas Hayward & Sons Ltd and the Falcon Works (Railway Signal Engineers.)

'REBUILT'-THE LETTERS AND COMMENTS PAGE(S)

This month's letters and comments starts with something bang up to date, so as far 'Southern Way' is concerned: the cover view of Issue 10, showing the pull-push set in BR red at Ventnor West.

Evidently we found something rather popular, as witness this letter from our regular contributor Viv Orchard, which arrived literally within a day or so of No. 10 appearing. "The striking cover picture raises two interesting points. There were two ex LB&SCR Push & Pull Sets on the Isle of Wight. Only this Set 503 had one of the drivers windows boarded in (or painted over). Why? The windscreen wiper appears to still be in place on the blanked out window. Also the coach end is fitted with lamp irons in the equivalent position of those either side of the smoke box on a steam engine, however the Isle of Wight engines did not have this facility. There is no plug for the electric head lamps so where they provided purely for the oil tail lamp?"

I was going to leave it exactly as above in the hope someone else might invoke a response but Gerry Bixley has kindly already done so, "Regarding the cover view of set 503, this is most definitely No. 4169, part of a two-coach set and regular on the line. Laid aside after closure, it did not find favour on other duties and was scrapped in the mid 1950s. The set had started life in 1911 on the Brighton - Worthing shuttle with three similar sets. Originally they all had sliding cab doors and were rebuilt with outward opening doors to the van: as were all IOW vehicles.

"The most unusual feature was the painted over glazing next to the driver's position. My guess is that this was because of the effect of a late departure from Ventnor West, facing the sun, which will definitely be in the driver's line of vision. No other vehicles were so painted. It is in unlined red, not applied to many vehicles.

"Jim Aston took some superb views of both vehicles in this set at Merstone on 18 April 1949. (See P101 of Mike King's 'An Illustrated History of Southern Pull-Push Stock'). The paint date was 1-49, Touch up and Varnish 1-50 and repaint and varnish 6-52. The 1-49 repaint had SR style set numbers (thicker than BR) and hand painted coach numbers, so I think your cover view depicts the 6-52 repaint, with BR set numbers and right-hand carriage numbers. I suspect the 1952 repaint was the first in red. *(In which case the view was taken in the closing months of operation as the Ventnor West line closed in September 1952 - Ed.)*

"By the way, a few years ago I came across a section of the van body of No. 4169 grounded on a farm on the Island. Unusually, the section had been grounded vertically, i.e. with the longitudinal panels facing up to the sky.

"The top view on page 4 (Issue 10), showing a lorry and trailer, is without doubt a demountable body. It may have been experimental, but again I am guessing. The trailer, No. 1065, appears to have been adopted with runners or rails for this purpose. Possibly a Thorneycroft."

Now further information on Tunbridge Wells West

from David Brown, "I found the article on TWW particularly interesting since I visited the signal boxes there (illicitly) a few times in steam days. Whilst clearly a Brighton station, it came under the Station Master at Tunbridge Wells Central. Similarly the relief staff were Eastern men who covered the two larger boxes at Tonbridge as well.

"It was generally considered that No. 1 box at 'Wells West', whilst the smallest of the three, was the most difficult. The problem was that very few trains ran through to Tonbridge and thus it was, in effect, a terminal station. Life largely consisted of the disposal of stock and engines and then remaking of trains for departures.

"When the DEMUs took over, many more trains ran through the single line to Grove Junction, which was worked by Staff and Ticket. However, when services were dislocated, the train staff could end up at the wrong end of the section. Since the single line section was only 860 yards long, the practice was for the two signalmen to walk towards each other and hand over the staff mid-section. This was fine until on one occasion when both men had convinced themselves that the other man had hold of and was bringing the staff, as result neither had! Soon afterwards, key-token, instruments were installed, which solved the problem once and for all."

Alan Blackburn now adds his own memories on Gerry Bixley's history of the C2 / C2X locomotives. "The Vulcans. These really were fine little engines. I first started on the railway as a box-boy at Fratton West in April 1952 and in those days a C2X was the normal engine rostered to haul the 12.15pm Portsmouth Harbour to Plymouth as far as Fareham: where the train would be attached to the service from Brighton. The stock was always a brand-new BR 4 set. The train would come under Fratton Road Bridge doing something like 45 mph

- what a sight. Today there is a Permanent Speed Restriction of , I think, 30 mph,, but in those days there were very few PSR's, these matters being left to the driver's discretion. The yellow cut out speed signs we take for granted today, were an LNER idea adopted nationally by BR in the mid 1960s.

"One other lasting memory of a Vulcan was in the winter of 1953/4. A 12 car train from Waterloo was stuck on the Down Relief outside the 'Town' box in about a foot of snow and requesting assistance. There was nothing immediately available until a 4COR from Victoria arrived in the Down Passenger loop headed by a Vulcan which had assisted it from Barnham. Mr Powell, the Station Master took charge of the situation, and decided that this combination should go in behind the Waterloo and assist it through to Portsmouth High Level.

"I do not thing anyone, excepting Mr Powell, was too hopeful of the outcome, but with a fantastic display of arcing and fireworks the whole lot did indeed get up on to the HL. One could have heard the Vulcan all over Pompey that evening. A few rules were disregarded, but what a fine example of co-operation between the three drivers.

"Someone mentioned the Brighton engines recently using their Westinghouse brakes to shunt or assist electrics. This was a common berthing practice at Fratton on summer weekends when electric stock was berthed in the Field sidings alongside the Goods Shed. E1 or E4's were the engines that were normally used. I believe something similar was done at Eastbourne."

We regret pressure of space means further correspondence - all appreciated of course, has of necessity to be held over to Issue 12 - *Ed.*

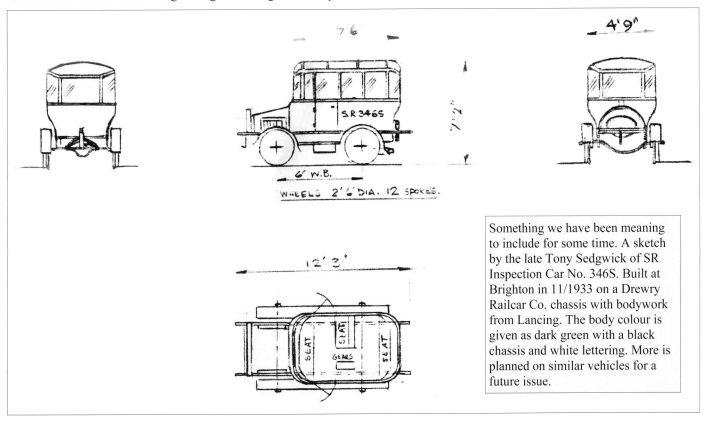

Something we have been meaning to include for some time. A sketch by the late Tony Sedgwick of SR Inspection Car No. 346S. Built at Brighton in 11/1933 on a Drewry Railcar Co. chassis with bodywork from Lancing. The body colour is given as dark green with a black chassis and white lettering. More is planned on similar vehicles for a future issue.

Crawley, photographed on 27 July 1968. This was the second signal box at Crawley brought into use on 31 March 1877. (An earlier box had been in existence from circa 1863 and was closed when this second box was commissioned.) Built to the LBSCR standard floor size of 15' x 11', the operating floor was some 16' from ground level, necessary to ensure good visibility of approaching trains over the station buildings. Within was a 21 lever frame at 5" centres, the levers having a differing pitch dependent upon whether they operated signals or points. Tappet locking was provided from an unknown date. A mechanical gate-wheel operated the adjacent level crossing until 5 February 1978 when lifting barriers were installed. The box worked until 20 April 1986 and survives today preserved by the 'Crawley Signal Box Preservation Society', whose aim is to restore it to its original state.
                                                                                                                                    John Scrace

SPOTLIGHT CRAWLEY

What is now the 100,000* strong thriving community of Crawley, had at the start of the 20th century been a rural backwater of just 500 people. Whilst it would be tempting to suggest the railway might be responsible for such growth, it could really only claim a part share, with some changes coming about in consequence of electrification of the route in 1938 but the major expansion subsequent to the Government's 1944 Abercrombie Plan, which proposed the establishment of 10 satellite towns around a 20 -25 mile radius of the capital**. The 'New Towns' Act was passed in 1946, by which time the number of proposed towns had also grown to 20. Despite objections and appeals from various landowners, all objections had been overruled by December 1947, shortly after this development of the area commenced, on what was officially deemed 'relatively poor quality' agricultural land. Aside from industry and related housing, business growth associated with the development of nearby Gatwick Airport occurred from the late 1960s onwards, concurrent also with the general trend of goods traffic moving from rail to road and consequent closure of wayside yards. (* - 2001 census.)

To return to railway matters proper, the line to Crawley had opened on 14 February 1848. Crawley then one of two intermediate stopping places on what was a branch line of the LBSCR running from Three Bridges to a terminus at Horsham. Eleven years later in 1859, the original single line was extended from Horsham southwards to Pulborough and then five years later still, in 1863, what had been a double set of rails from 1862, was extended still further to Arundel and a junction with the coast line at Ford Junction. For many years the designation, the 'Mid Sussex' line was used to describe the route, perhaps not exactly geographically correct, but still readily identifiable by many today.

Following electrification, the Southern pattern of regular interval services was provided, interspersed with steam hauled freight workings. At Crawley, the main goods facilities were on the up, or north side of the line, these were extended in 1938. east of the station, on the down side, was a trailing connection into the down siding, off of which was a gated private siding for Messrs. Longley - steam saw mills. Timber and coal would arrive at this facility, where there was also a short narrow gauge line, completed wooden floor blocks being sent out

by rail. A short bay on north side at the east end of the up platform was used mainly for parcels traffic.

Goods ceased to be handled sometime around the mid 1960s and the yard was closed. With the site then cleared, a new passenger station was constructed immediately north of the original site in the then fashionable, but austere pre-fabricated style. This new facility opened on 28 July 1968. Further progress occurred when lifting barriers were installed at the High Street / Brighton Road and Southgate Avenue crossings. From April 1986, MAS signalling under the control of the Three Bridges Signalling Centre has taken over control of what are now basic up and down running lines as well as remote monitoring of the level crossings.

(** Amongst the other places identified at the time as being potential 'New Town' locations were White Waltham in Berkshire, Chipping Ongar, Harlow and Margaretting in Essex, Stevenage, Stapleford and near Redbourn in Hertfordshire, near Meopham in Kent and Crowhurst and near Holmwood in Surrey. In addition there would be a dispersal of population from London to already existing towns including Ashford (Kent), Chelmsford and Witham in Essex.)

Right - 'Terrier' No 678 entering the station from the direction of Horsham.

John Scrace collection

Left - *Ford Prefect, and local Taxi on the up side frontage. The wooden structure on the right was 'Southern Counties Car Hire Service' - Telephone No. 'Crawley 1029', centre building with the drapes: unknown, and just in camera to the left, W H Smith. Notice the bicycle propped against the wall between the buildings, it displays the then common practice of a section of white paint on the rearmost part of the mudguard.*

Centre and bottom left - *The main station house and buildings, believed to date from the opening of the line in 1848. The views on these two pages were clearly taken on a warm summer day. It is believed the images were recorded circa 1959/60 period.*

Below - *Necessary peripherals and what also looks very much like a firing shovel.*

Both pages, Paul Hersey collection.

The publisher acknowledges with regret that it has so far been impossible to locate a track plan of Crawley. If a reader has such an item they might loan, we will willingly include it in a future issue of 'SW'.

SPOTLIGHT CRAWLEY

Right - *The up side buildings with what appears to be a narrower than usual platform. Southern railway green and white enamel signs predominate. From the finger post, a train for Three Bridges, Gatwick Airport, Redhill, East Croydon and Victoria is expected.*

Centre - *Weighing machine, long-case clock and Way Out / Waiting Room. Passenger access and exit to the platform was via the booking hall.*

Bottom right - *The down side buildings, this time with a train for Bognor Regis expected.*

Bottom - *Gentlemen's facilities were provided on both platforms, those on the up side at the east end of the main building near the footbridge: almost immediately outside of which was a seat. On the down platform there was a urinal underneath the actual footbridge steps.*

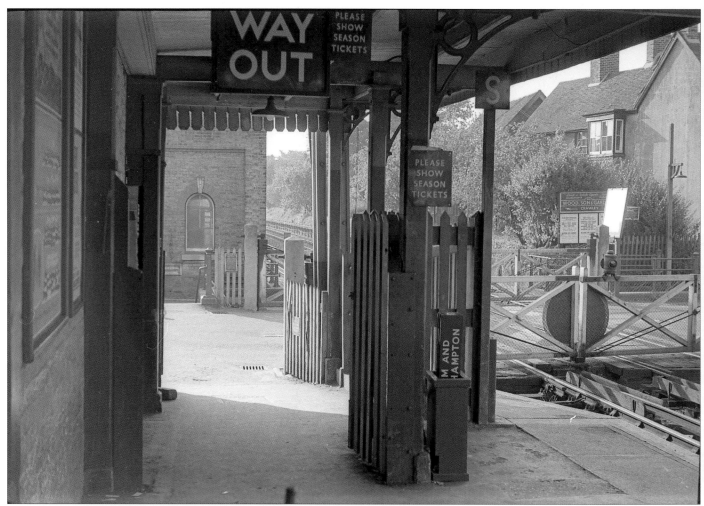

Opposite top - The south end of the down platform and station exit onto High Street / Brighton Road. The base of the signal box is also visible on the opposite side of the level crossing. At the base of the signal box can just be seen the steps that led down to a pedestrian subway under the railway.

Opposite bottom - The Booking Office entrance was behind the wooden fence on the up side. Local and national advertising is present.

This page, top - With a display of somewhat travel weary road vehicles in the background, we see the Station Master's Office. The Southern had several examples where the SMO building was detached from the main offices, no doubt in consequence of the need for extra space. Clearly not original, the date of its provision is not reported. Notice the 'double-ended trolley': see page 35, bottom row, second from right, visible. Behind what appear to be pigeon-baskets, an old LSWR brake vehicle rotted away at the end of the siding.

Right - 'D1' 0-4-2T No 269 carrying the name 'Crawley'.

J Scrace collection - 1, and Paul Hersey collection

SPOTLIGHT CRAWLEY

This page, top - *Through the station viewed east towards Three Bridges. The portacabin type building on the left was provided sometime about 1966 and whilst no doubt serving a necessary purpose cannot in any way be said to have improved the aesthetic appearance of what was rapidly becoming a shabby site. 27 July 1968.*

This page, centre - *Inside the footbridge. This was provided sometime after 1874 and was to a standard LBSCR design: a similar structure, although devoid of any roof covering survives at Chichester.*

This page, bottom left - *A second public footbridge maintaining a public right of way across the railway, was provided sometime after 1874 and provides for a good vantage point of the station from the east as well as placing in context the various goods facilities. The down siding connection is visible on the left. Early plans, indicate two sidings on the down side. One went into the yard of the Station hotel (seen behind the platform). It may be this was used for carriage trucks as there were likely to have been stables. The second went into a bay on the down side. 21 March 1958.*

Opposite page, top - *from ground level a variety of items are seen in the yard, including an 'Iron Fairy' mobile crane and what appears to be a semi-trailer used for carrying glass.*

Opposite page, bottom - *the 1938 siding extensions. It will be noted that it was only the main running lines and crossover that were electrified.*

J Scrace - 2, and Paul Hersey collection.

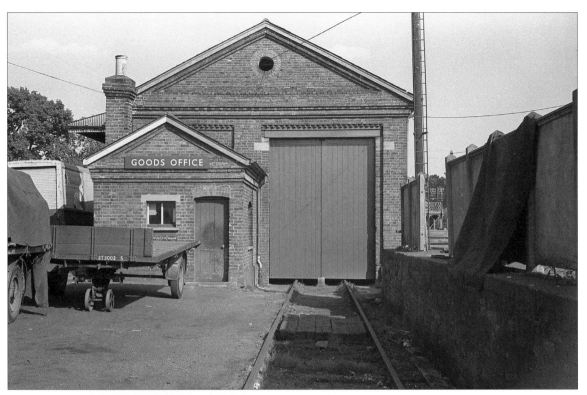

Good yard scenes., together with associated clutter. The exact purpose of the individual buildings, clearly provided over the years in a very much 'ad-hoc' manner, has not been established. With the presence of so many road vehicles, it is reasonable to assume that Crawley was perhaps a main depot for delivery to a wide area. Prior to urban development in the area, horses had been dealt with at the bay platform although by this time such traffic would be long gone. On early plans, on the west side of the yard, a short siding had curved away towards coal staiths operated by Messrs M Nightingale. The dates this operated are not known although Gordon Gravett recalls it as operational in the mid to late 1950s. The fixed crane seen had a capacity of 4.5 tons.

Paul Hersey collection.

This page - Yard detail at Crawley, very much a mixture of the old and the more recent. The two vans, bottom right, were marked for internal use at Crawley and would have been used as additional storage: albeit being moved around the site as required.

Opposite page, top - West of the station towards Ifield, a second public road crossing necessitated the provision of what was Horsham Road Crossing, also referred to as No. 7 Crossing. Opened in 1898, an earlier structure is known to have been provided, it survived until 1977 when barriers remotely operated from Crawley were installed. The hut had a frame of 5 levers and measured just 7' x 7' x 3'.

Opposite bottom - The west end of the new station, recorded on 27 July 1968 the day before it opened at which time the original station closed. The yard and associated buildings will be seen to have been demolished whilst there is no longer siding access to Messrs Longley: years earlier this firm had been responsible for the building of the stations on the Cuckoo line. The train is the 9.40 am Bognor to Victoria with Unit 2112 leading.   *J Scrace - 2 and Paul Hersey collection.*

(Further, colour, views of Crawley appear on pages 97-99. The assistance of Gordon Gravett in the compilation of these notes is acknowledged with thanks.)

~ MOMENTS ~

Above - Reedham Halt, on the Tattenham Corner branch, between Smitham and Purley. Written on reverse of the print is the note, "Bandits at Surrey Railway Station - Bandits attacked a railway office booking clerk at Reedham Halt, near Kenley, Surrey, and tried to remove a huge sum of money, there was a terrific fight." No date is mentioned, although clearly post 1928, (when the third rail was added), and giving the distinct impression of 1930s. Any more detail would be welcome. (Bandits? - sounds very 'wild-west'. 'Robbers' would be more accurate, - using or threatening that force would be used. I think we also have to allow for journalistic licence over the mention of a 'large sum of money' being involved. Hardly likely at a wayside stopping place.)

Left - Last day of the old station at Crawley, Saturday 27 July 1968. '2BIL' set No. 2069 leading an 8-car rake on a Victoria to Littlehampton service. No. 2069 was one of three sets comprising a motor coach of the type depicted here and a post-war all-steel HAL trailer. (The others were Nos. 2100 and 2133.

John Scrace

Terry Cole's Rolling Stock File No. 11
A TRIP TO THE ISLE OF WIGHT

In this issue we take a trip to the Isle of Wight, always a sanctuary for antique stock. All railway companies, especially the Southern, put old stock to further use if possible once it was withdrawn from front line duties, but the Island regime took this policy to new heights. This was due in no small measure to the difficulty of getting fresh stock to the island, which necessitated use of the floating crane. It was also assisted by the seasonal nature of its traffic which meant additional labour was available for maintenance in the winter months.

Opposite, top - In this view we see ex LSWR 44ft bogie passenger guards van resting at the buffer stops at Cowes. Built in June 1898 as LSWR No. 247, it was renumbered 4515 before becoming SR No. 241. In 1936/7 it was one of 9 similar vehicles transferred to the Isle of Wight and renumbered 1021. Seven of the nine were returned to the mainland in 1950 leaving just two, Nos. 1021 and 1022 which lasted until 1956. As we can see 1021 still retained its full panelling when this view was taken on 25/5/53, its sister vehicle had succumbed to having its panelling fully sheeted over by this time.

Opposite, bottom - This little vehicle, 1279S, seen here at Ryde on 25/5/53, and exhibits the IOW 'fully sheeted' style. It started life as LSWR passenger guards van No. 213 built in May 1892, later becoming No. 4482 and was one of many similar 30ft 6-wheeled vehicles built between 1888 and 1894. Eleven of these were taken into Eastleigh works between 1924 and 1926 and converted to 4-wheel vehicles with Westinghouse air brake for use on the IOW, taking numbers 995 – 1006. Gradually they were withdrawn as the 4-wheeled passenger trains with which they worked were replaced. Nos. 1000 and 1001 were converted to Breakdown Tool Vans in 1938 and numbered 1279S and 1280S. All the wooden mouldings were replaced with steel sheet and their origins became scarcely recognisable. 1280S. was allocated to Newport and was withdrawn in 1957. 1279S was based at Ryde and lasted until 1960.

This page - Now this is a really interesting vehicle. At first glance in appears as if it might be ex LBSCR but that is not the case. No.445S, seen here at Newport on 25/5/53, still carrying SR departmental livery, started life as Isle of Wight Central Railway No.3. This was a 7 ton Goods Brake and Tranship Van constructed at Newport with its twin No.2. The wheels and ironwork at least came from an earlier Stroudley vehicle and the body may have been a rebuild. Taking SR numbers 56035/6, old No.2 was withdrawn in 1928, however No.3 (56036) was converted to an Engineers Dept Tool Van No.445 S. in 1929. Usually based at Ryde, it lasted until some time in the 1950s.

[All photos author's collection]

WINCHESTER MEMORIES

Rodney Youngman

"Why don't you come up to the railway station? There are vacancies for staff": so said Fred Cooper, as he delivered parcels to Sheriff and Ward, the Winchester department store – nowadays Debenhams. Fred leant out of the cab window of his red and white Scammel 'mechanical-horse'; "See you there", at the same time starting to turn his vehicle right round in the narrow street. I later learnt Fred was an ex-GWR man, who years earlier had helped deliver material for the construction of the now closed Winchester by-pass, at the time considered the epitome of modern road design and construction.

I was then working at what was my first job from school, in the despatch department of the department store, dealing with parcels both in and out. Most of the former arrived by rail and were then delivered by railway lorry. Apart from Fred, there was another driver, Bert Britten, whom I called Benjamin after the famous composer.

What attracted me to Fred's suggestion, was that he had told me I would be earning far more than my current £4 a week wage: consequently it was not long before I presented myself to the Station Master's Clerk at Winchester City station. There I was issued with an application form by a formidable lady, who seemed to take some delight in advising me that, 'if I were successful, I could expect strict discipline.' I got the distinct impression that it was she who ran the station, not the actual Station Master!

Apart from being completed by me, my application form needed to be supported with the names of two referees – professional persons who would vouch for my good character. Luckily I was able to persuade my doctor and dentist to act as signatories. Having returned the completed papers, I was advised it would be forwarded to the Staff Office at Southampton for consideration. In

> Rodney Youngman spent 46 years working for the Southern Region and its successors, all of it based at what was originally called 'Winchester City'. Commencing as a Junior Goods Porter - in his own words, "...the lowest form of railway life…", he progressed through various outside portering roles to become a clerk in the Booking Office. Here he recounts his memories from some of those years, together with the individuals and personalities involved. Whilst clearly centred on Winchester, it is a story which, if the names and locations were changed, might well relate to any medium size Southern Region station of the period.

due course I was summoned for interview where I expressed a wish for a clerical post. To my disappointment I was advised there were no clerks' jobs available, but I could start as a Junior Goods Porter. I learnt later this was the indeed the lowest form of railway life, although I hoped it could become a stepping stone to a railway career, besides the pay was a princely £6 per week: Fred had been right.

Having passed the interview, I was told to report to the Goods Agent (the old term was still in use), at Winchester City on 27 September 1960. I was 18 years old.

Despite having already been in a working environment, I was till slightly nervous that first morning. Having confirmed my details, I was sent off to find Ernie Farrow, the Foreman in the Goods Shed. It was not a good start. I approached with a cheerful, "Hello Ernie, I'm the new Junior Goods Porter". He visibly bristled: "*WHAT* did you call me". I tried again, "You are Ernie aren't you?", I responded, already somewhat chastened. "To you, boy, I am Mr Farrow", placing a definite emphasis on the 'Mister'. "What's your name?" "Roderick Youngman – Sir", I now stuttered. He mellowed slightly, "That is far too long, from now on you will be known as Rodney". That same form of address would continue for my 46 years of railway service."

As the new boy I was naturally tasked with the menial duties. Making tea and lighting the coal fires in the various offices and mess room, the latter at the country (north) end of the goods shed. From the warmth of the cabin, I would listen to the sound of the exhaust from the engines as they set off towards Micheldever and Basingstoke. A soft chuff or the louder bark of the Western engines, the latter on Portsmouth to Reading workings. A cold winter's morning always seeming to magnify the sound more than in the summer months.

Half a century ago, the

Taking a break at Winchester in May 1963, the last year the 'B4' class were active at the station. (Their replacement for the remainder of the life of the goods yard was a 204 hp diesel shunter.) The engine has drawn up into the headshunt towards the Andover Road bridge, although as this was a dead end any thoughts of proceeding much further north, even with 'Class A' headcode discs, were unlikely! Nos. 30096 and 30102 left Winchester for the last time in the autumn of 1963, although No.30096 would have a further lease of life in private ownership at Southampton, renamed 'Corral Queen'.

Rod Hoyle

North through the station at Winchester, the designation 'City' was added from 26 September 1949. The goods shed referred to by Rodney is on the left, backing on to the up platform (nowadays referred to as 'Platform 1'). The seats, lampshades and tannoy system are typical Southern and would survive until the end of steam. Notice too the wind-breaks protecting waiting passengers who used the platform seats. In the lower view, a Urie 4-6-0 has charge of what the headcode implies to be Feltham duty No. 105. This was scheduled for a 4-6-0 running light on certain days and so this seen here may well have been an empty stock movement. Having left Feltham yard at 9.27 am, the engine was eventually destined for the 8.25 pm freight from Eastleigh to Preston Park.

goods shed (nowadays a car repair centre), was packed from end to end with packages for delivery around Winchester, whilst we received a similar volume for onward despatch. One of my jobs was to chalk the destinations on the wagons awaiting onward forwarding and so make for easier loading by the staff.

From the relative comfort of the goods shed, I was soon transferred to the goods yard proper, all of which again is now given over to car parking. At the time though there were sidings parallel with Andover Road, these running back around a sharp curve alongside Stockbridge Road. Outside, life was certainly harder, working in all weathers loading and unloading all manner of freight alongside the other goods porters. We were controlled by a fierce yard foreman, nicknamed 'Ginger', who certainly saw to it that we did not slack. As an example, I remember the day we were all huddled round the small stove in our mess hut sheltering from driving sleet when the door burst open and Ginger yelled, "Get outside you lazy b*****s and unload those wagons instead of sitting here warming your a***s".

As one we scuttled out to empty open wagons containing sacks of basic slag: a farm fertilizer. In the inclement weather our ungloved hands quickly froze as the sticky contents seeped from the saturated Hessian sacks.

Mention of the stove reminds me we used to purloin coal from the locomotive shed nearby to supplement our meagre supply. Unfortunately this steam coal was totally unsuitable for domestic use and the chimney of our fire became blocked on a regular basis. Fortunately the remedy was simply, a detonator tossed into the stove followed by a hasty retreat. The resultant explosion created a lot of black smoke and of course noise, but it worked every time. The permanent way staff, who we obtained the odd detonator from, were sympathetic to our plight: perhaps there was a common bond in that they too worked outside for long periods.

The adjacent locomotive shed housed a 'B4' 0-4-0T, No. 30096 or its sister, No. 30102. These were kept busy all day shunting wagons around, their modest size, compared with their main line brethren, belied their importance. One day, however, No. 30096 did have it moment of glory. The most important train of the day, the 'Royal Wessex' failed in the up platform. After much debate the engine was detached and No. 30096, affectionately known as 'The Bug', attached itself to the long line of now empty coaches. Amidst much wheel spinning the little engine began to pull the coaches forward for temporary storage in the sidings on the opposite, down, side of the station. The long siding here was always referred to as 'The Baltic', a reference to the men and supplies loaded here around WW1 destined for Russian ports.

The waiting crowds gave No. 30096 an almighty cheer as she gallantly completed her task, probably the only time in her life she was at the head of a named train. It was a sad day when No.30096 and her sister left Winchester for the last time, to be replaced by a diesel shunter. I stood on the platform with the regular fireman of No. 30096, Dave Yaldren, and waved a fond farewell. Dave left the railway shortly after-

wards, but was still a fireman – this time with the Winchester Fire Brigade.

The regular Winchester driver was Frank (his second name escapes me). He told me during WW2 he had driven ammunition trains into the forest near Longparish on the truncated remains of the branch from Fullerton.

Back at Winchester, this was the era when we started to receive small containers, forerunners of the much larger containerised freight of today. In similar fashion though, these first containers were designed to be lifted off a railway wagon and placed on to a railway lorry for delivery, the actual container having a hook at each corner of the roof to which chains would be attached, the whole then being lifted by crane. What was supposed to happen, was that I would climb on to the roof by ladder and await the crane. When this arrived I would attach the chains and then dismount by the same ladder. The container would then be carried to the waiting lorry – or from lorry to waiting wagon, and the same process, ladder – chains - ladder, repeated.

But this was time-consuming and so to save precious minutes, when the crane approached, the jib would be lowered and I would place one foot in the chain and by holding on to the jib be hoisted on to the roof of the container. Here I would attach the chains in the usual way and then cling on as the container was carried to the waiting vehicle. At this point the procedure was reversed.

Winchester had at this time a shunter by the name of Bill, well known for his perhaps less than careful attitude to work. One of the places Bill would shunt wagons to and from was the actual goods shed, at each end of which were two large green doors, closed at night for security. One morning the early turn porter, whose first job was to open these doors, was late. Bill was on duty, but without bothering to check, he simply waved the engine forward as it propelled wagons with freight arrived for Winchester. The result was one set of doors were reduced to matchwood. On another occasion I was at the Stockbridge Road end of the yard aware there was a gap of about two wagon-lengths between the last wagon on the siding and the buffer stops. In the distance I could see Bill waving the engine back that was to take the afternoon pick-up goods. To my consternation he just kept waving it back and back. Slowly the wagons moved towards the buffer stops until there was no space left, at which point they hit the buffers and rose majestically into the air. I was powerless to intervene. Shortly afterwards Bill was moved to platform duties.

One attribute of Bill though, was that he was ever the wit. One day an imperious lady traveller held up a sixpence and said, pointing to her suitcase, "Put that on the 3.30 for me". Bill was quick off the mark, "Yes ma'am - but what horse?"

For my own part I recall the day when we were unloading some sharp implements, one of them dropped on to my finger and blood poured from the wound. The foreman wrapped a bandage around it and then said, "Now you can get back to work". Even today, 40 years later, the nail on that digit still causes trouble and is painful.

Eventually I was moved back inside the goods shed

The sharp curves of the goods yard are typified in this view taken from St Pauls Hill. Originally this part of the yard had been served by wagon turntables but these were replaced with that seen in the latter part of the nineteenth century. The corrugated engine shed dated from around 1928. Two railway road vehicle trailers are visible as well as bolster wagons carrying steel. This particular traffic going from and to Messrs Condors at Winnal.

and promoted to completing the delivery sheets for the drivers. It also came to the notice of the railway authorities that I had legible handwriting, with the result I was offered a post in the parcels office on the passenger side of the railway, now earning £8 a week. My mentor was Graham Hawkins, who had started on the GWR at nearby Worthy Down. Graham was a superb instructor and steeped in the traditions of the GWR. He would have made an excellent clerk but preferred instead the 'uniform' side of the railway. He smoked his cigarettes through a long holder, which gave him a rakish air. Due to having bad feet, Graham was allowed to wear plimsolls rather than the regulation black shoes. This gave rise to the nickname 'Bootsie', after the character in a popular television series of the time, 'The Army Game'.

Graham came from a railway family: his brother served in the Railway Police and his father had been a ganger on the DNS line at Whitchurch where they had once won the annual award for the best kept length of permanent way on the London Division of the GWR.

On one occasion Graham was summoned to the Station Master to explain why an entry in the station diary stated,

"Graham Hawkins reported drunk on duty." Graham explained it was not he who had been inebriated, but instead he had apprehended a drunk who had alighted from a train somewhat worse for wear. Another amusing entry was, "Whilst I was carrying a parcel from Winchester to Liverpool, it fell on the track".

Humour could also be found in some of the announcements made by the Station foreman, Charlie Davies. Charlie took his position very seriously, but did not always think before he spoke. One winter's day he was told by control to warn passengers to take care due to the icy conditions. Accordingly when the train stopped, he announced in his Hampshire brogue, "Be careful when you get off, else it might be a bit slippery, look". Another time, he commented that he had been unable to obtain the wanted information from control, "The down Birkenhead is very, very late. As a matter of fact nobody knows where it is". His counterpart, Cecil Hook, used to announce the Mid-Hants branch trains as calling at Hitchen Habbas, Halresford, Ropley, Medstid and Orlton". Cecil's brother, Gordon, also worked on the railway and had transferred to Winchester after the Romsey to Andover line closed. For years he had

The summer of '62. A Standard 'Class 5' heads north with a Reading parcels working, passing No. 30096 paused between duties alongside the p/way hut at the north end of the up yard. The grinding stone was an essential part of the p/way equipment, used for sharpening rip-hooks which the men would use to cut grass on the cuttings and embankments.

been his own master at Horsebridge and found the transition to a busy station quite a shock, however we worked well together in the parcels office.

In the 1960s, the office was still very busy, with a great deal of traffic conveyed by rail. We had a special lorry delivery just for Woolworths as there were so many regular parcels for them. In total there were three railway vehicles working from the station, two delivered in the city area and one that dealt with the villages in the surrounding countryside. All the mail-order firms, Kays, Great Universal Stores, and The Empire Stores, sent their goods by rail for their customers.

Each morning, the newspapers would arrive on 'the paper train', Winchester being split between two major delivery agents, Wally Wheble and Pete Davidge. (I still see Pete today as he is an avid supporter of Winchester City Football Club and I am a Club official.)

Another early morning task was to sort out the boxes of fresh fish which had travelled overnight from Grimsby. At that time one of the local fishmongers was Mr Anderson, who had a fresh fish shop in Andover Road near the bottom of Station Hill. One of the sadder items we received were boxes of guinea pigs from Porton destined for what was then the animal centre at Martyr Worthy. I recall we were told we must never touch or handle the creatures.

The most bizarre item I received was in late 1963. A man, Dennis Whitty, had been jointly convicted of the murder of a Cornish farmer and sentenced to hang at Winchester Prison. His partner in crime, Russell Pascoe, was executed at Bristol gaol at the same time. Already a gallows had been erected in the prison yard and the day before the execution we received an oak box addressed to 'The Governor, H M Prison Winchester – from the Home Office.' Due to constant handling over the years, there was a hole in the top of the box.

Curiosity overtook any feelings of guilt and I put my hand inside: it was the hangman's noose! One would have thought it would feel like any other rope but it was thick with grease and felt like a steel hawser.

The next day, large numbers of protesters arrived by the trains and made their way to the prison to form a vigil for the miscreant, incidentally the last man to be hanged at Winchester Prison. Ironically, 100 years earlier, the LSWR used to run excursion trains to Winchester for spectators to watch what were then public executions. Such events were then considered 'a good day out', and whilst awaiting the 'highlight', the crowd would be entertained by jugglers, clowns and other performers with refreshments provided, washed down by beer. Returning to 1963, shortly after 8.30 am, a lorry from the prison brought back the aforesaid box for return to London.

In my time in the Parcels Office, it was still possible to send a corpse by passenger train. I never actually did – but I did receive one. An elderly lady from Winchester had died whilst on holiday in Durham and it was decided to return her body by train and the coffin was placed in the parcels van of one of the through trains from the north. On arrival at Winchester and after the ordinary passengers had both alighted and joined the service, the train pulled forward so the parcels van was drawn up immediately opposite the door to the Parcels Office. Here we waited with a large luggage trolley on to which the undertakers loaded the coffin and then pulled the trolley to the waiting hearse.

In the outward direction, and apart from the mundane parcels, we had some unusual packages. One was live eels from the River Test near Stockbridge, packed in wooden boxes and destined for the London East End markets. One day someone dropped the box, the lid flew off and dozens of the eels were writhing on the parcels office floor. Our best efforts to

The circus comes to town. 'E2' No. 32101 shunts the Bertram Mills circus vans from where they had arrived in the up side and across the main lines into the down sidings at Winchester. The 'E2' has just emerged from Eastleigh Works, having been the last member of the class to have retained Southern livery. Circa 1951.

Eric Best

Bottom left - Not Winchester of course, but considering the story of the elephant on the opposite page, it seemed the ideal illustration to include! The location is in fact Lyndhurst Road and clearly another circus occasion. The date was not reported.

Mark Abbott

Bottom right - Seen from Andover Road Bridge looking south, this is the down side yard with the cattle pens, the warehouse of Messrs. R G Gifford 'Coal, Corn and Seed Merchants': this firm also had another warehouse in nearby Staple Gardens, and in the distance, the spurs leading off to further sidings, coal staiths and at the far end, an end loading dock. The bridge from which the photograph was taken had two arches. One for the up and down main lines, and a second on the left, of single track width - hence the narrowing of the track into one line at this point. This single set of rails continued north under the bridge running parallel with the main line for some distance and was, and indeed still is today, referred to as the 'Baltic' siding. For almost 40 years now it has been the solitary remaining siding at Winchester.

Another member of the 'B4' class, No. 30093, seen at Winchester on 28 March 1960. Just hidden behind the loco is the ground frame which operated the crossover allowing access to and from the yard and main line. It was electrically released from the signal box. No 30093 has clearly been pressed into service by the p/way gang and is carrying a number of sleepers complete with chairs at the base of the smokebox.

South Western Circle / Eyers Collection

pick them up were in vain as they slipped from our grasp. Then someone had an idea. There was a consignment of Hessian sacks awaiting delivery to the West of England Sack Company at Bar End. We took out a few from the bundle and this rough material enabled us to recapture the elusive creatures.

Other livestock we handled were the favourite hounds of Sir Brian Mountain, who owned a country estate at nearby Shawford. He would send the animals by train, although while they waited they would be safely ensconced in the parcels office. Unfortunately they would bay and cry so loudly we found it difficult to carry on a conversation with our customers. Consequently we were glad when they had gone: although Sir Brian used to reward us with a side of venison every Christmas.

Another time there was a large ram to be sent away for breeding. It was placed on a trolley direct from the lorry and in this way wheeled across to the opposite platform by the board crossing. Here, and with great difficulty, it was lifted off and tied by its collar to a nearby stanchion. When the train arrived, the van was placed immediately opposite, but the ram had decided he was not going to move and no amount of tugging, cajoling or threats was going to make him change his mind.

The train was also by now already delayed and we had almost abandoned our attempts, when a young woman waiting for the next service approached us. She must have been watching our behaviour with some amusement as with the words, "That's not the way to do it, I own a sheep farm and the only way to make him move is to do this....". She bent down, placed her hand under his tail and squeezed something soft in that vicinity. The ram shot in to the van and it was immediately, "Right away Guard".

More gentle creatures were young calves. They would arrive with their legs tied together to prevent injuring themselves and, with only their heads protruding out of the top of a sack, were clearly in distress. I learned that by giving them my thumb to suck they would soon quieten down.

We also dealt with racehorses, sent from a local stud for breeding and always destined for the North of England. This required arranging in advance, so telephone contact was made with Wimbledon for a suitable horsebox, bearing in mind the eventual destination. The empty vehicle would arrive on a parcels working and be detached and shunted by the 'Bug' into the cattle pen on the down side. When the horse arrived for loading, I would place the appropriate destination labels on each side of the boxes together with a supply of hay and water. The 'Bug' would then take the vehicle across to the siding alongside the goods shed ready to be attached to the up working. It was also our job to advise the destination station that the vehicle was on its way and make arrangements at various points en-route for the fodder and water to be replenished. In the case of a particularly valuable animal, a groom might also travel in the special compartment.

I recall the circus arriving by train at Winchester, probably one of the last occasions the railway was used for this type of traffic. The route from the station was lined with spectators as the animals left the Andover Road side to walk to what were usually the playing fields. 'Dinger' Bell and myself had been detailed to clear the cattle pens of any deposits left in the course of unloading. 'Dinger' though was a bit quick off the mark and started work before the animals had departed. Consequently as he bent down to scrape up some elephant dung, jumbo seized the shovel in his trunk and flung it high in to the air. We scattered, as both it and the contents hurtled to the ground.

During my time in the parcels office, I dealt with plants, and sometimes even trees, sent by Hilliers, the respected horticulturalists. These might be consigned to all parts of Europe by train. I became the person responsible for the correct charging as well as preparing the correct documents for customs and border controls. According to weight, I would

65

need to consult charts to convert Sterling into Francs, Marks, Drachmas, Roubles and the like. It even ended up with me receiving calls from other stations enquiring as to the procedure for sending parcels abroad.

Another traffic was racing pigeons, sent from fanciers in the Midlands and North. We had to be careful not to release them during inclement weather or close to telephone wires. The empty baskets would be returned to the sending station with the day and time of release recorded on the label.

Being close to the growing area, we dealt with watercress. This came from the growing beds at Springvale and would arrive by tractor and trailer which we would always hear some time before it arrived at the station. The cress was packed into small raffia baskets called 'chips'. They were mainly destined for markets in London, Manchester, Portsmouth, Brighton and Hastings. Because of the perishable nature, we had to work out where the connections would be and

telephone each transfer station to ensure the chips were off-loaded on to a connecting train. Frank was the usual tractor driver, but if he was not available, we would receive a call from the staff at Springvale to warn us that Miss Stringer, the owner, was the way by car. Woe betide us if the trolleys on which the watercress was due to be loaded were not ready immediately opposite the doors to the parcels office. With dire threats as to what would happen if the cress was delayed en-route, this fearsome lady would be gone almost as soon as she arrived. I remember there was a flat-rate charge of 6d for the conveyance of each chip. Nevertheless, we always received a couple of bunches of the delicious cress for our troubles.

Sir Arnold Laver was a well known timber merchant with many mills in the North of England. He owned a country estate at Preshaw and liked his own fresh fruit and vegetables from his farm to be sent to Sheffield whenever he was on business there. He employed a retainer, a rather blunt Yorkshire-

Left - No. 34060 '25 Squadron' entering the station at 3.00 pm on Saturday 31 July 1965. At first glance this would appear to be Bournemouth duty No. 357, a limited stop service from Waterloo. However, the 'A' class headcode, rather than the Southern Region route code discs, and presence of non SR stock, would infer this was in fact an inter-regional service.

Right - Having set back into the 'Baltic', Standard 'Class 4', No. 76033, restarts away south, with down vans for Brockenhurst and Bournemouth West, routed via Wimborne. 19 October 1963.

Both - Tony Molyneaux

man, who would bring in the hamper of produce. Anxious that nothing would go wrong to displease his master, he would say, "Make sure that basket goes on the 'Master Cutler' from London." This connection, via London, gave the fastest service from Winchester at the time. I would have to telephone Waterloo to make sure the hamper was placed on the regular lorry service that inter-connected the various termini. Throwing a 6d on to the counter, he would leave, confident in the knowledge that his generous gratuity would ensure his demands were met.

One day Sir Arnold himself came into the office accompanied by his man. After requesting his hamper be placed on the train on the basis, "...wife's waiting for it". He placed a half crown on to the desk. "Nay master", responded the assistant, "he only gets 6d". With a wry smile, Sir Arnold departed, still leaving the 2/6d where it lay.

There were other renowned customers as well: one was Viscount Cunningham, Commander in Chief Naval Forces in the Mediterranean during WW2. He would send apples from his orchard to his equally famous brother, General Sir Alan Cunningham.

From time to time we would be visited by the railway auditors, very strict and meticulous in their examination of the accounts books. When we despatched parcels, we affixed a parcels stamp to each package, rather like a postage stamp: these ranged in value from 1d to £1. I remember being asked once why the issue of 1d stamps on a particular day and which should have totalled 10, actually showed that 11 had been taken off the pad? I was unable to explain the error, other than I must have stuck two on the same parcel. The result was I was required to complete an 'Irregular Use' form – in triplicate. Despite this, they must have been pleased, as at a later date it was the same auditor who recommended me to take the examination to become a booking clerk, of which more anon.

At Winchester, our Accounts Clerk was Miss Green, who had joined the railway in WW2. Known to all as "Nellie", she was a small woman, with round 'NHS' type spectacles which added to her spinster-like appearance. She also always seemed to wear the same green cardigan. One would never have dared address her by her first name, but in return she addressed all the staff in similar respectful manner. Miss Green was the daughter of a railway guard, whose train had been stopped in the tunnel at Southampton during an air raid in 1941. When the 'all-clear' sounded, the train started with a jolt and Guard Green was thrown against the brake capstan in the van breaking his back and necessitating his early retirement. Nellie was thus the sole breadwinner for the family. She was famed for her knowledge of the most obscure regulations con-

'Merchant Navy', No. 35021 'New Zealand Line' in the sidings at Winchester having come to grief with a broken coupling rod. The date was not reported: the men were Eastleigh fitters sent to take down the motion in readiness for movement to Eastleigh and the requisite repairs. (It is not known if this was the engine on the failed 'Royal Wessex' working referred to in the text.)   Mark Abbott

cerning parcels traffic, but one day even she was flummoxed when the request was for the movement of a 3-wheeled invalid carriage, with motor attached, to Eire.

To seek advice she contacted Headquarters, but after a delay, the man at the other end came back with, "We haven't a clue, why don't you phone the parcels clerk at Winchester - he knows everything". Somehow between the two of use we concocted what we believed to be a realistic charge, confident in the knowledge that no one would be able to contradict us.

In the parcels office we also dealt with left luggage and so looked after everything from an umbrella to a motor cycle. When the Winchester College boys went on weekend leave they were in the habit of chaining their bicycles against railings or posts. One boy was apprehended by a porter and told to take his steed to the left luggage office. Annoyed, he said, "How much is it to leave my bogle here until Sunday?" I knew the boys had their own school language and a 'bogle' was their own term for a bicycle. He was advised the charge was 2/6d, which elucidated the reply, "What, Great Scott, that much"? Throwing a coin on to the counter he continued, "Make sure that goes in the till. I don't want you to quaff ale with it when you go off duty".

Another of our tasks with lost property was trying to telephone the next stopping point of the departed train on which some unfortunate passenger had left their belongings. If the search was unsuccessful, we would have to write a 'UTM' or 'Urgent Train Message' to each subsequent stopping place for the service. A particularly onerous task if this was a stopping train to Weymouth with perhaps 20 calls en-route.

One day a young lady came into the office crying. She said she had lost her engagement ring. On enquiring of its last known whereabouts she admitted she had thrown it on to the track following an argument with her boyfriend. Fortunately the item was located glistening in the ballast.

Nowadays with the hype surrounding unattended bags and other items, passengers are told to leave any unattended item well alone, but years ago I recall one Sunday just after a

down train had left, that there was an unattended lady's handbag on one of the platform seats. As per regulations, I fetched another member of staff, in this case 'Topper' Brown. Together we checked inside, which, apart from the usual paraphernalia, contained £200 in notes, a considerable sum back in the 1960s. Shortly afterwards there was a call from Eastleigh, enquiring if a bag had been found. On confirming its safety, we were told the owner's husband would return to collect it. I reminded the staff at Eastleigh that a note from the owner permitting me to release it was necessary. When he collected it, I stated that it had been checked with a colleague and because £200 was in the bag, a lost property fee of 2/- was payable. "We were uncertain how much was in it", the husband responded, "If you had taken £20 out we would not have known. Such honesty should be duly rewarded….". With that he paid the 2/- and put a further 6d piece on the counter. I had to share this with 'Topper'.

I remember a young lad was appointed as railman at nearby Shawford which in those days still dealt with a small amount of parcels traffic. Consequently we were required to give him some basic training. The day he started he received a call from a 'Farmer Giles'. "I'll be bringing my pigs up tomorrow to send to Ireland. Have everything ready, including the documents and tell me how much I have to pay". Shortly after our telephone rang with a panic stricken voice at the other end. The laughter he heard soon alerted him to the fact he was the recipient of a hoax.

Working on a Sunday, I had to cover both the ticket collectors' lunch and tea breaks in between my parcels office duties. My memories of the regular men on these duties also stand out: Arthur Apps, Jack Nelson and the infamous, 'Jock' Simpson. No-one ever passed Jock without showing their ticket or pass. A man who had been at Eastleigh Works for years was on first name terms with him. One day there was the customary, "Good Morning Jock / How are you Jim?" exchange, followed by, "Fine, but my pass is in my other jacket, luckily you know me". "You'll have to go home to get it", was the stern response. "But Jock, you know I live in Kings Worthy and will be late for work if I have to go back". The response was even firmer, "Too bad. You are not passing the barrier. I won't let you through" - and he didn't.

Once, Jock's wife arrived off a train from Southampton where they lived. She told him she had been issued with a privilege ticket despite leaving her identity card at home. Jock duly excessed her ticket up to the full public fare.

Jock had previously worked in the left luggage office at Southampton Terminus. On one occasion a merchant seaman left a suitcase for a few hours and when he returned opened the lid and gave Jock 50 cigarettes as a tip. Jock noticed the suitcase was packed only with cigarettes and watched which train the seaman boarded. He duly alerted the railway police and a smuggler was apprehended.

We also had a German ticket collector, Henry, who had anglicised his original name of Heinrich. Henry had served in the German Navy in WW2 and was captured when his U-boat was sunk. Later he decided to remain in England as his home city of Leipzig was occupied by the Russians. Unfortunately a relief clerk sent to Winchester, noticing Henry was on duty, goose-stepped across the ticket hall and gave a Nazi salute. Nowadays such action would lead to disciplinary action

and probable dismissal, but poor Henry had to simply grin and bear it. Henry told me that as a boy he had been a reluctant member of the Hitler Youth, but it seemed that occasionally the old days still came into his mind. One of these was when a member of the right-wing British National Party had been incarcerated in Winchester Prison and many anti-fascist demonstrators arrived for a demonstration rally outside. As he observed the hordes passing through the station complete with banners, there was a hint of nostalgia in his eyes as he observed, "Those fellows are nothing but agitators, in my day they would have been put against a wall and shot." Henry's mother lived in the eastern part of Germany and on the rare occasions he went to visit her he often had problems at the border crossing between east and west. He told me of once when the border guards had stripped his car of its seats, doors and other parts in a search for contraband goods. Finding nothing amiss, they simply left it to Henry to reassemble it all again.

I used to do the odd turn of overtime duty on the platform to supplement my wages. The time I liked best was when the Hampshire DEMU units arrived on the terminating service from Southampton Terminus. In order to get the train to start its return journey from the opposite platform, the driver would remain in one cab and propel the set into the up siding. I would

35010 'Blue Star' on the Up line, passing a 'Mogul' waiting in the down platform at the head of a lengthy parcels working. In the foreground are the south exit from the goods shed and the goods-shed by-pass roads; the headshunt for which terminated at the Romsey Road overbridge. At one time there had also been a trailing connection into the up main line from the goods yard at this point. With the 1967 extension of the platforms at Winchester to accommodate 12 coach trains, all signs of this headshunt has long since been obliterated.   *Rod Hoyle*

We make no excuses for this being closely similar to, (but certainly not identical) to another Rod Hoyle view of Winchester reproduced in an earlier edition of 'The Southern Way'. Aside from affording a delightful impression of waiting luggage, the tickets collectors booth on the down platform and metal sliding doors leading to the platform - all of course now long since swept away, there is a glimpse at the ticket hall and Booking Office. Winchester only ever had one booking office, on the down side, passengers for services travelling north having to use the steps and subway to reach the opposite platform.

be in the rear cab and after the unit had cleared the points, dismount to press the plunger which advised the signalman the set was in and clear of the running line. The dummy would then come off, I would climb into what was now the front cab, give the driver at the other end two rings on the internal buzzer and we would make our way the short distance into the down platform. En route I would usually find an excuse to sound the horn whilst also changing the red blanks to the train number.

My time in the parcels office was coming to an end. I had passed the clerical examination and was appointed to a position in Winchester Booking Office, subject, that was, to successfully completing the six-week ticket office course. This was held in a series of huts at Lower Marsh, below Waterloo. The course was intense but thorough and included an examination on dealing with parcels, necessary as some clerks at the smaller stations would have this in their remit as well. This was an area where my previous experience helped and I was obviously delighted when told I had passed to the requisite standard.

So, I reported for my first day of duty at Winchester, expected also to learn from the more experienced clerks over the next few weeks. As the junior I also had the more mundane duties, sharpening pencils and general housekeeping duties. I was also expected to address the chief clerk as 'Mr Puckering', only the senior clerks called him 'Peter'. Similarly the then Station Master was always Mr Chalk or even 'Sir'.

Eventually I was considered competent and ready to 'take on'. It was 1967 and fortunately with far fewer ticket types: 'Ordinary Single', 'Ordinary Return', 'Cheap Day Return' and a 'Forces Weekend Return Ticket', the latter in consequence of the troops then based at Peninsula Barracks -

nowadays a housing development. We would also receive from the military a list of ticket requirements in advance, something which saved much unnecessary queuing.

When I started there were still the wooden racks around the office walls containing tickets to the most popular destinations and of course numbered sequentially. These were held in alphabetical order with the lowest issue number at the bottom – this was so we could easily calculate how many of each had been issued. The bottom ticket left after an issue was always pulled half way out, so that its number was exposed. That way we knew at least one ticket from that stack had been issued. Each week, and later every month, we would 'take-off' the numbers and with the aid of a 'ready-reckoner' book, calculate the grand total. For example it might have been 177 Cheap-Day returns to Aldershot at 7/11d (£70 1s 3d). These figures would then be entered in the various ledgers together with income from other areas, platform tickets, car and motor cycle parking receipts, ticket collectors' receipts, income from 'cab-tolls' – the charge levied to taxi operators authorised to ply for hire at the station, as well as a myriad of other miscellaneous sources. Naturally it all had to balance, the figures then being sent on to the accounts office at Waterloo. The actual cash and cheques (no plastic card payments then) were banked each day by Mr Puckering, taking one other clerk with him for security purposes. Later on, Winchester was selected as being one of three stations to act as a 'guinea pig' when plastic first came to be used with paper transaction slips. The other locations on the Southern Region were, for the Central Division; Haywards Heath: and at Canterbury West for the South Eastern Division. Having resolved any problems over card payments, the system was rolled out throughout the region.

Should we not have a printed ticket available, we would make recourse to a 'blank-card'. This had Winchester City printed on the top. Unlike the standard issue tickets in the racks which had the fare written on a gummed label underneath the rack, recourse was instead made to the 'Fares' Book'. This was a vast volume of many pages in which prices to various destinations by differing routes were hand written. The destination station and route were recorded in ink but the fare was in pencil, so the same page might be used when there was a price increase. At times people would also purchase a ticket for travel after a price increase was due to take place and which meant there was the complication of needing to have two separate Fares' Books in use at the same time.

Worse still was when someone might ask for a ticket to a little used station, such as Flamborough, between Hull and Scarborough. Reference to the book would show that no fare was recorded and so now a geographical knowledge of the railway system became essential. We would calculate the fare on the basis of the route to be used, in this case adding together the distances in miles and chains between the various stations and junctions: Winchester – Reading West Junction – Banbury – Nottingham Victoria – York – Scarborough, and finally to the destination station at Flamborough. The total was rounded up to the nearest mile making 303 miles at 9½d per mile giving a fare of £11 8s 3d.

We also had books of 'paper tickets'. One of these was red and used for group travel where a large number of perhaps adults and children might travel together to the same destination. The other was printed in green and used for 'Private Settlement', such as a shipping company or combined bus and coach tickets. It saved the issue of perhaps 100 or more individual tickets.

I particularly liked writing a ticket for Cowes, Isle of Wight. Where my colleagues would write in the 'via' column, 'Red Funnel Boat', I would print in small letters 'via, The Southampton , Isle of Wight and South of England Royal Mail Steam Packet Company Limited'. Another was, 'To Portsmouth Town Station, London & South Western and London Brighton and South Coast Joint Railway', or 'Weymouth Town Station, Great Western Railway'. I once received a group booking for the regatta at Henley on which the suffix 'GW' was shown and another group to 'Ascot LSW'.

The Edmondson cardboard tickets were dated by holding the ticket between forefinger and thumb and inserting it into the date press. You could always tell if a man was a booking clerk as the constant pressing of the ticket in the slot at the top of the press left a permanent ink mark and indentation on the knuckle of the thumb. Tickets issued for travel in advance were dated with a rubber stamp. Supplies of tickets came in bundles of 250, secured by string which took a certain art to release. With the span of one hand, grasp the ends of the bundle whilst the other hand cut the string. If the grip was released for a moment, tickets would fly in all directions and you were left with the laborious job of restacking them in the correct numerical order. Each evening the date in the ticket press had to be changed ready for the next day. This involved extracting the

tiny pieces of type and replacing them. Again great care was taken to avoid disaster. If a piece fell on to the floor it could take an age to find.

Each Thursday saw the release of those who had served their time at 'Her Majesty's Hotel' – more accurately Winchester Prison. They were issued with a travel warrant to return home but in the interests of economy, we were instructed from the Home Office to use the cheapest route. Usually the released person was anxious to get home as quickly as possible, so the caveat 'via London' or suchlike was a common addition, invariably in rather crude writing. Anyone who presented one of these was quickly turned around and sent back to the prison for a replacement, unaltered, warrant. Then there was the cheeky Irishman who handed over a warrant for travel to Belfast with the words, "This is for First Class on the boat train from Euston to Holyhead and a First Class cabin on the boat". He was given Second Class via Reading. One outstanding memory was when a Scotsman gave me a warrant for a journey to Glasgow with the words, "I'm not going home, I'm only going to Southampton, so you know what to do." "What's that?" I replied. "Give me a single to Southampton but put the cost of the ticket to Glasgow on the warrant". Then take the difference out of the till, you give me half and half for yourself. That will be about £30 each." "Goodbye", I said, "this warrant is cancelled."

I recall another ex-prisoner who arrived at the ticket office with his warrant, wet through. I expressed my sympathy having had to walk from the prison in a rainstorm, but he replied, "You wouldn't mind what the weather was if you had just come out after 12 years for murder."

Sometimes, after a ticket had been issued in consequence of the travel warrant, the recipient would bring it back, usually to a different clerk, and ask for a cash refund. The reason given being that they had bought it in advance and would not now be travelling. What they did not realise was that a printed mark on the ticket showed the method of payment.

Another problem with fraudulent claims was when the claimant was particularly obnoxious. A member of the Salvation Army or other charitable organisation might bring with them an allegedly penniless individual and purchase a ticket so the unfortunate might be able to reach either home or a town where there was a night shelter. The ticket would be purchased for cash although once left alone the holder would then try the same refund trick with another clerk. We had our own ways of dealing with such situations, like writing on the ticket itself 'No refund permitted.'

Moving forwards a few years, it was not just the travelling public who would try to buck the system, some railway staff would try it on themselves: one such example was at the time of decimalisation in February 1971. In connection with this changeover, £1 coins were issued in brown paper rolls containing twenty coins. An auditor told me one of the stations he visited, (he did not divulge the name), had a large amount of coinage allocated as a float. Being short of space they kept about 10 of these rolls on the top of the shelf, such that it required a ladder to reach them. Because of their position, it became the custom of the auditors to glance up, count the rolls and multiply the sum, to total £200. My conscientious friend, on his first visit, decided to fetch a ladder and do a physical count. On picking up the first roll it was nowhere near the weight it should have been – quickly explained that the 'rolls of coins' were in fact pieces of sawn off broom handle. Another time he was called to a station due to a theft. When the early turn clerk had opened the safe to extract the float, all he found was empty space. His float, together with the takings from an Easter Weekend: Good Friday through to Easter Monday was missing. Another clerk from the same station was the culprit, although true to his calling, he had made life easy for the auditor by leaving a list of what the safe should have contained!

Talking of safes, I was at Shawford for a week, which station safe was opened, not by the usual combination lock, but by means of a key almost a foot long. On opening the door, there was on the inside a beautiful coloured emblem, "By Appointment to her Majesty the Queen". This wonderful piece of Victoriana, probably dating from when Shawford was opened in 1882, mysteriously disappeared when the station became unstaffed.

The incumbent railwayman, on leave when I covered his duties, was not known for the diligence in carrying out his job. With the sparse service of stopping trains, although non-stop workings were at times seemingly almost continuous, I decided to clean up what was a rather untidy station. I swept the platforms, the station approach, put up new posters and cleaned the windows. The landlord of the adjacent pub, 'The Bridge' even came out and remarked it had been three years since this had been last done and to 'Watch out' as I would be for it when he returned. Sure enough, next week the telephone rang, "If you ever come down here again, leave things as they are and just issue tickets".

I got a better reception at Basingstoke where I would sometimes help out on a Summer Saturday morning. It was exceptionally busy, especially with bookings to the West Country. I would also on occasions work at Eastleigh and Southampton Central.

One clerk, who would sometimes cover relief at Winchester, would have a fast response to any number of questions. When asked, "Do you sell tickets to Cowes?" he replied, "Yes madam, and to humans as well."

We were required on occasions to cover in what was then the new Travel Centre at the station, giving out bus and local tourist information. I preferred though the hustle and bustle of the ticket office so returned there when the opportunity arose. I was also now working with a former clerk from Romsey who had come to Winchester on promotion. He recounted the story of the family who arrived at Romsey to start an onward journey to their holiday destination at Exmouth, necessitating changing trains at Salisbury. Unfortunately the Romsey to Salisbury service was running 10 minutes late and meaning it would miss the connecting service from Salisbury to Exeter. Consequently he called control advising them and asking that the Exeter service be held to avoid the family having an hour's wait at Salisbury. 'Control' was brusque in its re-

sponse, "In no circumstances will the West of England train be held back." "Very well", said the clerk, "I will advise Lord Mountbatten and his guests accordingly…" The Exeter train was held.

In connection with the Bournemouth electrification, the booking hall at Winchester was renovated, and as Winchester had once been a Roman City, so the architects decided to model it on a Roman temple, complete with arches over the ticket office windows and columns supporting the roof. Gone then was the wooden floor – where a coin had been nailed down. We would take great delight in watching, when after a furtive glance, someone would bend down to try and pick it up. Elsewhere on the station there was a desk in the foreman's office due to be removed which had remained locked for years: no one knew where the key was. We prised open the lid to find, a dead rat, several pieces of part chewed paper and a wooden gas-rattle, marked 'S.R.'. I claimed that for my own collection.

The W H Smith bookstall was also demolished around this time, but I was not so lucky with some of the artefacts there. These were taken away by an enterprising builder, and included pre-WW1 newspapers and posters.

As with any working environment it was the staff who made it what it was. Two of the members of the permanent way department come to mind here. The first was Phil North, a small man who always wore a 'pork-pie' hat. As a young man he had been trialled by Arsenal Football club, but unfortunately WW2 intervened. Even so he could skilfully juggle a tennis ball and kick it in a dead straight line into an upturned bucket. The other man was Ernie Gibson, whose weakness was for carrying out practical jokes. Once when in the station buffet he asked the attendant if they had a certain item. It was on the top shelf requiring the use of a ladder to fetch it. Having carried it down, Ernie said, "I only wanted to know if you had it."

Ernie used to cycle to and from work. After carrying out numerous pranks on his workmates, they decided to get their own back. Ernie went to get his bicycle but instead laid out in front of him was a tarpaulin – his machine had been taken apart down to the last nut and bolt.

We had a station cleaner, Mrs Rose, whose job it was to keep the offices and waiting rooms clean and polished. When I worked in the parcels office she would arrive with two cups of tea, one for each of us. She would then sit on a stool next to the fire and doze off, having said, "Wake me up in 20 minutes – Cedric". (another variation on my name.)

Undoubtedly the most memorable man was our station master, Mr Walter Gilbert, known to all as 'Olly'. He was a Midlander who had once been a signalman at a box near Nuneaton. He recalled the terrible blitz on Coventry in 1940, having been told to report information to control if he spotted enemy aircraft. Olly was a man of few words, so all he said was, "They're coming". Once when he was going to be late home he called his wife and said, "I'll be late, have pie ready at nine". He did not even greet her or say who he was. He was a brilliant operating man but did not like the commercial aspect of his work. He would sign the monthly accounts but only do a few checks, trusting us completely. We did not let him down.

WINCHESTER MEMORIES

The station master's clerk once told me the story of John Arlott, the cricket commentator who burst into the office demanding we stop the non-stop Southampton to Waterloo service as the preceding train from Winchester had been cancelled. "Can't do that, it's on its way", said Mr Gilbert. "I demand that you stop it!" replied Arlott. By now riled, Olly said, "What do you want me to do, stand in the middle of the line with a red flag? You will have to wait for the next one." Poor Olly, he was always nervous when someone of importance was due at the station. On one occasion he was told to accompany Princess Alexandra from the ticket hall to the London train. She duly arrived with Lord Mountbatten, who, after kissing her goodbye, left. Mr Gilbert approached her and said, "I'm sorry, Your Majesty's train is half an hour late". Not perplexed by his faux-pas over the form of address – it should have been 'Your Royal Highness', she put him at ease by responding, "Never mind, Station Master, if you would care to get me a cup of tea from the buffet we can wait in your office" - a truly gracious lady.

Other remembered station masters were, Don Baker, Harry Newman and perhaps the best all-round man, Bernie Briggs, who knew every aspect of railway work from A to Z.

Of the sadder memories, this relates to Harry Hiller. Harry had been a GWR man at Lambourn, Burghclere and finally station master at Whitchurch, the latter station renamed 'Town' and passing to Southern Region control in 1950. It was rumoured you could see your own reflection in the polish on the floor of the waiting room at Whitchurch. No one would dare sully it. When the station at Whitchurch closed, Harry was transferred to Winchester, as station master's clerk. He, though, saw it as demotion and although carrying out his duties diligently he did not mix with the staff, although I did get on with him. On his last day before retirement, some of us went to his office to say farewell. The door was locked. Harry had slipped away unnoticed.

Early in my booking office career, there was a visit from the General Manager of the Southern Region. In those days, the most senior positions on the railway were usually taken by ex-army officers. It was felt that as they were used to dealing with men, they were ideal candidates for these important jobs. This GM was an old-fashioned disciplinarian by all accounts. When he came into our office, accompanied by the station master, we were all duly lined up for inspection. First our chief clerk was introduced and shook hands, followed by

An unusual visitor to Winchester on 2 June 1956. No doubt in consequence of the non-availability of a 'B4', 'C14' No. 30588 was recorded acting as pilot at Winchester on 2 June 1956. It was reported that the engine was attaching an extra vehicle to the 12.05 pm, Alton - Eastleigh service.

Top left - No. 35011 'General Steam Navigation' attracting the attention of some youthful spotters as it arrived with a Bournemouth / Weymouth working. 31 July 1965.

Top right - No. 34048 'Crediton' awaiting departure with the 10.20 am to Waterloo, 19 October 1963.

Bottom left - For some time in the autumn of 1963, No. 34102 'Lapford' was the regular engine on the up and down 'Pines Express' workings, running from Bournemouth via Oxford. Normally this a rake of maroon BR coaches, although under a glass, the seventh vehicle back may well be a green Bulleid vehicle. The backs of the houses are on Brassey Road, after the 19th century railway builder.

Bottom right - Newly rebuilt and on a running-in turn, No. 35014 'Nederland Line' leaving north, 15 July 1956. This was one of six members of the class, modified in that year.   All - Tony Molyneaux

Opposite page - Following the closure of Winchester Chesil for goods, City Station dealt with remaining coal traffic. Here 'Class 4' No. 80140 arrives with wagons for the yard after which it will return light to Eastleigh. 20 September 1966. Notice the conductor rail is now in position.   South Western Circle / Eyers Collection

my fellow clerks: they were addressed as 'Mr'. Then I stepped forward. "This is Youngman, the junior clerk", stated the chief clerk. My extended hand was ignored and the GM, pointing to the ticket window simply stated, "Carry on".

It was inevitable that in my 39 years in the booking office some famous faces would appear wanting tickets or information. One was the much loved actor, James Robertson Justice. He would seem to act in real life exactly as per the roles he portrayed in the 'Doctor' films. He lived in Stockbridge and every Monday morning would buy two first class tickets to London. "One for me and one for my niece" – said with a twinkle in his eye. He must have had an extraordinary number of nieces - all of whom bore a remarkable resemblance to the young actresses who appeared in his latest film.

One night Susan Hampshire just missed the London train. She spent the next half hour chatting to me about films and life in general. Loraine Chase, famous for her one time adverts encouraging people to travel to Luton Airport, once bought a ticket, but I resisted the temptation to ask the obvious question as to her destination.

Among sports people we served were David Gower, conspicuous by his mop of blond hair, and Graham Souness the football manager, always immaculate in a pin-stripe suit. If there was a long queue he would wait quite patiently, yet always found the time to pass the time of day. Other notables were Martin Bashir, who lived close to the station although my favourite encounter was with the actor Edward Fox. One night when I was on late turn, I noticed a figure in the ticket hall. No one else was about, all the other passengers from the recent down train from London having left the station. The man came towards me, and I immediately recognised him as the actor, "Good evening, I wonder if you would be kind enough to direct me to the Theatre Royal". I advised him accordingly, to which he responded, "Thank you so much. Perhaps you could confirm the time of the last train to Waterloo?" Again the character of the person came through, a gentleman both in the roles he plays and also in real life.

From Andover Road bridge, 28 March 1960, before rationalisation and redevelopment.

South Western Circle / Eyers Collection

Pre nationalisation Winchester.

Top *- An unidentified Drummond 4-4-0, seemingly with steam to spare on a special working to Crystal Palace.*

Bottom - *Another unidentified engine, although clearly a member of the 'King Arthur' class. The engine is awaiting departure south. Notice the end of the headshunt referred to previously.*

Howard Butler collection.

Rodney Youngman - from a photo feature of several members of Winchester staff that appeared in a local newspaper in 1969.

....and following....

Hugh Abbinnett's own reminiscences of work at Winchester Shed...

Tales from the Smaller Sheds - 2

Hugh Abbinnett

Unlike at the main depots, life "in the country" could be very different indeed. Just seven miles north of the main depot at Eastleigh also on the main line, was the tiny locomotive shed at Winchester. (Not to be confused with the smaller station but bigger shed at Winchester GW.) Here on the Southern line was out-stationed a diminutive locomotive, necessary because of the sharp curves in the yard. These were not able to be eased due to housing development. In my time it was always a former LSWR type, invariably a 'B4', although stories, but alas seemingly no photographs exist of trials involving a South Eastern 'P' type and even a Brighton 'Terrier'.

As a young cleaner and then passed cleaner at Eastleigh, it fell to the likes of my grade to cover should the regular Winchester night steam-raiser be absent for any reason. But management were also aware of the behaviour of us younger men and so to ensure all might be dealt with satisfactorily should we be sent on an 'away-day' - perhaps 'away-night' might be more appropriate - it was the practice for the Eastleigh foreman to send two of us to cover the one vacancy at Winchester.

Thus it was that one night two of us from Eastleigh, 'Ike' Till and myself, found ourselves riding with the smartly turned out Passenger Guard of the up 'Night Mail' ready to be turfed out at Winchester. The fact I was at the time just 15 years of age and thus supposedly not permitted to work before 6.00 am, was of little consequence to management. It was probably more of a concern to the Guard, our loco-stained overalls ready to sully his own compartment: he was polite but wisely kept us at a literal arm's length.

At this stage it should be explained that when the local man was away, it was the practice to throw out the fire of the little 'B4' at the end of the day, the rationale being that the locomotive could then be safely left unattended. It was thus to this situation that the two young cleaners arrived in the darkness of the small hours and cautiously opened the large doors of the shed. The eerie sensation was not helped by their knowledge of the presence of a graveyard backing on to the rear of the shed, and the lack of any available artificial lighting inside.

We had brought with us the necessary kindling, wood, paraffin, lubricating oil and cleaning cloths for their own use, most carried by myself, Ike as senior man, using his position to dictate accordingly. Despite the fact the engine had not had a fire within for several hours, it would still creak and snap and groan as the metal contracted, this was enough to cause alarm to us both, especially within our present environment. Plucking up courage though, we started work, placing the various loads on the footplate before the important job of lighting the flare lamp. So, whilst Ike gave out instructions re the kindling, he trimmed the asbestos wick and lit the end. The result was an immediate white glow - enough to once again startle, although at least now we could see what we were doing. Importantly also, from the light of the lamp we could see there was water in the gauge glass but as suspected, no fire left in the grate, although it at least still pleasantly warm.

Pieces of wood were then placed into the firebox, lumps of coal added and a little paraffin poured over the top. Using a carefully selected sliver of wood, Ike lit this as a taper, waiting for it to burn properly before tossing it into the firebox where the releasing gases immediately lit with a gratifying 'woof'. Now we could shut the firebox doors and wait, sitting on the seats on either side of the footplate, the conversation soon turning to locomotive matters with Ike explaining his superior knowledge as to how to make the locomotive move, but also seeking re-assurance that the time they had available, 2-3 hours, would be sufficient to make sufficient steam, ready for when the Winchester crew arrived for work. If we had but known, the accompanying creaks and groans now emanating from deep within, were the very signs we had been waiting for, an indication that the developing heat was causing the copper and steel to expand accordingly.

Checking the fire at intervals and adding small quantities of coal from time to time, it was with considerable relief when there was the first signs of the water starting to move up and down slightly in the glass, a sure indication that the water was 'on the boil'. Soon afterwards came the initial movement of the needle on the pressure gauge.

The instructions they had been given at Eastleigh were explicit, 'raise steam, nothing else.' But having succeeded in raising sufficient steam, we both saw no harm in perhaps moving the loco just a little, outside of the shed - "perhaps to fill up the side tanks", although a quick examination revealed these had been topped up the night before. The decision then reached, was to move the engine out of the shed, "to make it easier for the Winchester men for when they arrive". Little could we have realised the repercussions that were going to occur as to both of us the rules did not matter. (The rule was an engine must only ever be moved by a Driver or Passed Fireman.) So by releasing the handbrake, eight turns were required, the engine was placed the in gear and after a very slight opening of the regulator, a few short puffs from the chimney had them stopped in their intended position. Here we again secured the engine on the handbrake, feeling rather pleased with our achievement and awaited what we honestly believed would be a grateful Winchester driver.

The regular Winchester man was called Frank. Due to a badly smashed leg, he had retained the Winchester job as he was unable to easily reach the higher footplate of the main line types. As such he regarded his employment as sacrosanct, his engine, his job: the thought of two 'kids' driving his engine was nothing less than criminal. Thus when the showdown came, in the hours before 6.00 am, Frank showed us no mercy, threatening to inform the Eastleigh Foreman of our misdemeanour. (With our tender service this would likely have led to the sack.) The situation was only calmed with the arrival of the first can of tea brought by Frank's fireman, and it was two considerably chastened and crestfallen cleaners who later boarded the train from Winchester to Eastleigh. Somehow, in the next few weeks, and despite the story becoming more widely known, nothing more was said, although more stories did begin to emerge of the strange goings on at Winchester during the small hours. Such as the time the little shunting engine chugged though the yard in the small hours with the whistle constantly blowing - but no one would ever admit to that.

Nestling quietly in the shed at Winchester - sub shed of Eastleigh, is 'B4', No. 30102. Recorded by Rod Hoyle in early 1963.

In the second of an occasional series of 'Might Have Beens', Peter Bailey examines Bulleid's 'Ugly Duckling' - *which fortunately, never got out of the egg.*

Normally, when one considers a locomotive that was designed, but never built, one expresses regret. But in this case, perhaps not.

The development of the Pacific idea on the Southern Railway has its origins in early experience with the Lord Nelson 4-6-0s, the first of which had entered service in 1926. Put simply, they were fine in the same links as the King Arthur class, but when pushed to provide the extra that was needed to increase the weight and reduce the timings of the Dover and Folkestone boat trains, they were not quite up to the job.

Initial disappointment was followed by experiment and modifications, notably the fitting of slightly smaller, six-foot three-inch driving wheels to number 859 and, later, a substantially enlarged boiler to 860. Mr C.S. Cocks, in his paper to the Institute of Locomotive Engineers, some years later in 1948, suggests that neither did a great deal for the performance of the Nelsons. Others have suggested that that the real problems were a firebox which was difficult to handle and a congested front end. Bulleid addressed the latter with some success but the problem with the firebox, which was one of handling a grate, flat at the rear but sloping at the front, was not overcome.

Maunsell's further attempt to provide boat train power was to design a Pacific, which would have incorporated the changes made to Nos. 859 and 860 and the inclusion of a firebox which, although still part flat, part sloping, would have been broader and shorter and therefore easier to fire. But the Civil Engineer said "No", as he would say a year or so later to a proposed 2-6-2. This brings the story up to 1934 and nothing more was to happen until Oliver Bulleid appeared on the scene in 1937.

Bulleid was an avowed steam man, but had been appointed to a railway which was looking towards electricity for major development. It had, in Mr. A. Raworth, an electrical engineer who, although technically junior to Bulleid, was enthusiastic and competent and had encouraged the Board to share his enthusiasm for this genesis of power. The new CME therefore faced an uphill struggle in developing further major steam locomotive designs beyond the drawing board. He also came from a railway which had made a big thing of streamlining. On the LNER he had been very close to Gresley and had probably had some small say in the development of streamlining after 1934. He was clearly a pro-streamlining man and this was going to colour his future thinking.

It is therefore no real surprise that Bulleid attempted to air-smooth a Schools class 4-4-0 and no sadness derives from the fortunate decision to drop the idea. The locomotive looked truly dreadful. There followed outline schemes for streamlined Pacifics and 2-8-2s and non streamlined locomotives of the same wheel arrangements. His streamlined proposals had none of the flair that was to be evident in the Pacifics. But the financial climate and state of the Southern's permanent way were against him and all of these ideas were put aside.

Water colour paintings of the Maunsell 2-6-2 and Bulleid 2-8-2 designs appear in Robin Barnes's fascinating book "Locomotives That Never Were", published by Janes in 1985, but for some years out of print.

Then came the war and with it all the stringencies that one would expect to accompany locomotive design and development. It is well known that surprise, bordering on incredulity, greeted the decision to produce what was clearly a 4-6-2 passenger locomotive during the those dark days, not long after Dunkirk, when the country had its back pretty close to the wall. It was air-smoothed too! The word streamlined was unofficially forbidden. The explanation that the cladding was to lessen the task of keeping the engine clean carried no conviction. But it was in this form that the first batch of ten locomotives was built. They ran, mainly at the head of express passenger trains and were not a great success with freight. That they were impressive and on a good day could work extremely hard and run fast soon became apparent. In truth, this dramatic addition to the locomotive stock of a major railway company was probably just what an overworked and demoralised transport system needed.

It is the second batch of ten Merchant Navy Pacifics that is represented in the accompanying drawing. Two pieces of information have been published, both in H.A.V. Bullleid's biography of his father. One is the weight diagram of an unstreamlined version of the Pacific locomotive. The other is a photo of the wooden model, built by Eastleigh craftsmen, shown to Bulleid and put aside on aesthetic grounds. The year of all this was 1943, by which time the first ten Pacifics were in service and the Q1 0-6-0s had also made their mark. So the un-streamlined locomotives would, one presumes, have been numbered 21C11 to 21C20. One wonders whether they would, initially at any rate, have carried names. Maybe streamlining and names would have come with the peace, a few years later. The drawing does show a nameplate, more to cover a rather dreary expanse of Q1 type cladding than from a conviction that it would be there.

Amongst the advantages of this revised, stripped down design would have been some loss of weight and easier access for maintenance purposes. How much weight would have been saved is an open question. One of the things the weight diagram does not show is axle loadings! Also omitted are major details, like steam pipes to the cylinders. The ones on the drawing are conjectural.

And, post 1946, would they have appeared in malachite green? I can envisage them in plain, wartime black, but somehow not in the post war colour. We shall never know.

To my mind the Bulleid Pacifics, in their final Southern Railway form, were good to look upon. I am glad that, in the event, they built them all as they did.

B.R. 31037

BRITISH RAILWAYS

SOUTHERN REGION

Notice No. 802.
AGM(T)
1961

NOTICE

OF

ROYAL TRAIN

VICTORIA

TO

TATTENHAM CORNER

ON

WEDNESDAY, 31st MAY, and FRIDAY, 2nd JUNE, 1961

This Notice must be acknowledged immediately by use of the enclosed form.

WEDNESDAY, 31st MAY, AND FRIDAY, 2nd JUNE—continued.

Formation of 12.10 p.m. Victoria to Tattenham Corner

ENGINE No. 30926 (" Schools " Class).

Gangways to be Connected
- Pullman Car " Isle of Thanet " (Brake leading).—For Railway Officers.
- Pullman Car " Aries " (Kitchen leading).—For Royal Household.
- Eastern Region Royal Saloon No. 396 (Saloon leading).—For H.M. The Queen.
- Pullman Car " Niobe " (Brake trailing).—For Servants.

EMPTY TRAINS :—

	arr. a.m.	dep. a.m.
Stewarts Lane	A	11† 9
Victoria (Platform 15—South Section)...	11†20	...

Form 12.10 p.m. to Tattenham Corner.

A—The engine to work the 12.10 p.m. " Grove " Victoria to Tattenham Corner to be attached to the rear of the 11.9 a.m. empty from Stewarts Lane.

H.O. Inspector Parker will travel with the empty train from Stewarts Lane to Victoria.

Formation leaving Stewarts Lane:—

ENGINE

Gangways to be Connected
- Pullman Car " Niobe " (Brake leading).
- Eastern Region Royal Saloon No. 396 (Saloon trailing).
- Pullman Car " Aries " (Kitchen trailing).
- Pullman Car " Isle of Thanet " (Brake trailing).

Formed of 12.10 p.m. Victoria.	arr. p.m.	dep. p.m.
Tattenham Corner	...	1†46
Kingswood	1	53
Chipstead	1	58
Smitham	2	3
Purley	2	7
East Croydon (Loop to Local Line) ...	2	15
Windmill Bridge Junction	2	16
	(Local Line)	
Selhurst	2	19
Streatham Common	2	26
Streatham...	2	28
Tulse Hill	2	32
Herne Hill	2	36
Brixton	2	38
Stewarts Lane ... ... ,... ...	2†48	

TRAVELS WITH MY CAMERA
David Chalmers

Wednesday 31 May 1961, Stewarts Lane depot. 'Schools', No. 30926 'Repton' is being made ready for a Royal Special from Victoria to Tattenham Corner. Posed alongside the engine are (Left to Right) Running Foreman, F. Bourner: Chief Mechanical Inspector, J. Stevens and Locomotive Inspector Danny Knight. Bert Woods was the Shedmaster of Stewarts Lane at the time. (See also additional comment at the foot of page 84.)

The rolling stock for the trains on the two occasions referred to opposite, was the same as had been used two weeks earlier on 17 May, when the Queen and Royal Party had travelled from Waterloo to Guildford for the consecration of the new Cathedral. On that day the locomotive had been No. 34009.

This page - A gloomy day at Stewarts Lane - although without reference to the working. The headcode only indicates a main line trip to or from Battersea and Redhill / Brighton. 20 January 1962.

Opposite page, top - Returning milk empties running through Overton, 12 August 1961 behind No. 34062 '17 Squadron'. This was one of two daily workings returning milk empties to the west country. For some years it was normally the province of a 'Merchant Navy' working back to Exmouth Junction. The siding trailing into the up line on the left split into a pair of lines off which was a lead into the private Portal's Siding. Here would arrive material for Portal's paper mill, where bank note paper was produced. The view is looking back towards Oakley, the next named location to be reached by 34062, the station at Whitchurch. Assuming the train was running to time, it would now be around 5.40 pm. The service was due to pass Andover Junction at 6.00 pm and similarly shown as passing Salisbury at 6.27 pm. Which of course asks the questions, as the train commenced at Clapham Junction and the final destination was Exeter Central, where did the locomotive stop for water?

Opposite page, bottom - The same day, sees a Salisbury duty for a decidedly grubby No. 34059 'Holsworthy', running through Overton with a Waterloo - Salisbury - Exeter service. In 1959, Overton was served by eleven down trains on weekdays, nine on Saturdays and just two on a Sunday. In the up direction, there were slightly fewer weekday trains, but some of these were limited stop between Salisbury and Overton and then omitted the Oakley stop before Basingstoke. Up trains on Saturday showed one more service than in the down direction, but again just two trains on Sunday. With the station having a reasonable amount of morning and evening commuter traffic (workmen and office staff for Portal's), this arrangement meant that those arriving from the west could enjoy an alternative to the all-stations stopping service.

Continued from Page 83 - David Chalmers recounts a amusing anecdote Mr. Stevens had told him concerning Danny Knight. Apparently he was very fond of beer (what railwaymen of that period were not?) and arriving on the platform at Waterloo for a train to Eastleigh, he entered the restaurant car and ordered a pint. "I'm sorry sir," said the steward, "I cannot serve you until the train is on the move." Danny was not to be denied. He immediately went up to the locomotive and asked the driver to move the train back and forth (what reason he gave is not recorded) and the driver duly complied. Danny returned to the restaurant car and looking the steward in the eye said, "O.K. the trains moving, I'll have that pint." The steward's reaction is also not recorded.

Opposite top - No. 30901 'Winchester', near Ashurst Junction in charge of the 4.40 pm London Bridge to Brighton service. It was noted the engine was carrying what was distinctly the wrong headcode. 23 August 1961.

Opposite bottom - No. 30928 'Stowe' at Grove Junction, Tunbridge Wells with the fireman about to surrender the tablet for the T/ Wells West - Grove Junction section. The train is the 6.05 am Brighton to Tonbridge and Redhill. 24 June 1961.

Above - The unmistakable outline of a 'Q1'. This particular example, No. 33019 seen eastbound near Gomshall. 22 July 1963.

Right - In consequence of the Kent Coast Electrification scheme, an inspection saloon is propelled through Paddock Wood on 10 June 1961, by BR '4MT' tank, No. 80067.

Opposite top - 'H' class 0-4-4Ts, Nos. 31543, 31308 and 31005 in varying states of (dis)repair inside the shed at Tunbridge Wells West, 17 March 1963. The centre engine, No. 31308 had been withdrawn at the end of 1962, but the others would soldier on into the summer of 1963.

Opposite bottom - 'E1' No. 31067 and 'D1' No. 31739, arriving off the Hawkhurst branch at Paddock Wood. The engines had taken a hikers' special from London to Cranbrook and were returning to Tonbridge for servicing. 28 May 1961.

This page, top - Tonbridge shed, with 'N1', No 31822 and an 0-6-0 diesel mechanical shunter. 17 June 1962.

This page, bottom - An awful lot of effort for not a lot of weight. 'Q' class 0-6-0 No. 30533 near Tunbridge Wells West en-route to collect a more substantive train. 17 March 1962. As an aside, two weeks earlier at the start of March, all the SR's fleet of BR Class 4MT 2-6-4T locos had been stopped following the discovery of cracks in some of the pony trucks.

Left - Ash Junction: the old route via Tongham seen on the left. 'N' No. 31870 has charge of a Guildford bound service.

Bottom - With five months of operational service left, 'H' No. 31522 stands outside the shed at Tunbridge Wells West, 10 August 1962.

Right - 'Q' No. 30544 at Groombridge with an ultra short freight for Brighton, 11 November 1961. The signal box was a BR replacement, opened 23 November 1958, for three other boxes in the area. It lasted until January 1969.

Bottom - The LCGB 'Wealdsman' railtour of 13 June 1965. Here a 'U' and an 'N' are featured, No. 31803 leading, with No. 31411 inside. The tour had started from Waterloo behind No. 34050 which took the train to Redhill via Horsham. Here the two engines seen took over to run to Heathfield, Hastings, Eastbourne and back to Haywards Heath. Then it was the turn of No. 34050 again from Haywards Heath via Steyning to Horsham, before 'Q1's Nos. 33027 and 33006 took charge of the final leg to Guildford and thence via Cobham back to Waterloo.

Top - *An unidentified 'N' class 2-6-0 on the Tonbridge - Redhill route, passing over the Oxted to East Grinstead line at Crowhurst, 13 May 1961.*
Bottom - *On 10 June 1962, 'Class 4', No. 75069 is near Birchden Junction with the 10.28 Victoria to Brighton working.*

Permanent Way Notes by Graham Hatton
Southern Railway Switch and Crossing Evolution
continued

Switches.

New standards for Bullhead (BH) track were drawn up by a group of senior engineers from the various companies near the end of the First World War and were published by the Railway Executive Committee (REC) in 1924[1]. At the time they were largely influenced by the GWR and adopted by most of the new companies after the grouping of the railways. However the GWR, despite its involvement, went its own way after this, continuing to develop its own standards, particularly evident in its different switch design. The Southern decided to embrace the new design immediately.

Switches and Crossings (S&C) last a long time, typically 25 years at this stage, so pre-grouping standards of S&C would still have survived after this date for many years before the track saw renewal using these new standards.

Switches are the moving part of the turnout: they comprise the two switch rails which are machined to a fine point at the switch toe and two stock rails on the outside. They are handed by standing at the toe position, looking towards the turnout's crossing. The switch and stock on the left are referred to as the left hand switch and stock rail etc. In 1924 the new standards were developed for switches A to F in Bullhead (BH) rail, with A being the slowest speed.

Photo 1, right. (Botley)

Although this photo shows a recent BH turnout at Botley near Eastleigh from what was originally the Bishops Waltham Branch, now a siding, it is being used here to illustrate some of the key items of the design of a set of switches as used by the Southern. Here it is a right hand BH turnout with 'C' switches, but the comments below also apply to subsequent Flat Bottom (FB) turnouts. These switches have recently been renewed so they show the fit of the switch and stock as it should be.

All switches are described, as mentioned in a previous article, by a number of factors such as hand, planing style, joggled, undercut etc. When the switches became due for renewal, information about the existing switches would be gathered and often the new switches would still replicate the existing situation, but using the latest standards to improve on a previous design style.

The point of this illustration is to show how switches are 'handed' left or right.

Only a very few are truly split switches having equal diverting radii to both routes through the turnout. Handing is most easily identified by standing on the plain line about 20ft / 6m in front of [2] the switches and observing, by looking along each rail towards the switches, which switch has a kink immediately in front

of the switch known as a 'set'. These switches have the set in the right hand stock rail and are therefore right hand switches. The set is important as the switch rail (straight planed in this case) gains thickness relatively quickly. Therefore to avoid excessively long switches, which would be caused by allowing the stock rail to naturally curve away from the straight line, which in turn would create very thin, long switches at the toe, the set allows the switch to become thicker and hence stronger more quickly at this vulnerable position. It is less obvious in longer switches, but the principle still applies.

The set which defines the hand of the switches is in one rail only, (except in the rare split switches, where a smaller set is in both stock rails). The set, as shown here, allows the switch to maintain a straight edge, parallel with the opposite stock rail at the appropriate track gauge. This angle of divergence is replicated in the opposite left switch as it gains thickness parallel with the right stock rail (the adjacent left hand stock rail is straight with no set) and this will give a 'lurch' when the left hand switch is shut, as the train is diverted from a straight route to negotiate the curve of the turnout. Longer switches clearly reduce this effect, and improved switch planing and fine entry switches were developed to further improve this, but there is always a set on one side defining the hand of the switches.

In a few locations the hand of the turnout may differ from the hand of the smaller component of the switch. This is best shown at the end of a loop line where the only route for a train is to regain the adjacent running line by a crossover.

Typically the loop line will end in a sand drag or buffers, for the route beyond the crossover points. In this situation,

and again considering the loop to be on the left of the running line, all trains will cross over from the loop to the running line via the crossover and it is hoped none will continue into the stop block. The crossover will normally use right hand turnouts; however the switches of the turnout in the loop only would receive heavy wear if they too were right hand, as trains passing would effectively grind away at the left hand switch tips as the wheels were diverted to the crossover route. In this case left hand switches are used, even though beyond the toes they look like right hand ones, the difference being the set is in the left hand stock rail and looks like a minor misalignment towards the main line (there is no set in the right hand stock rail, it simply curves to the right). The effect of this is to divert the flanges approaching the switch and thus the following left hand switch sees less sidewear at the tip. These switches would be referred to as 'left hand switches curved right hand', the rest of the turnout would look like a normal right hand turnout. The SR design office used this policy in many locations and its still in use today.

It is a small detail, but Permanent Way, like all railway items, relies on detail like this, found from experience to improve the life expectancy of, in this case, the switches.

More details on the complex geometry at this point is beyond the scope of this article, but the details are published in British Railways Track and other publications mentioned in previous articles.

Photos 2 and 3 (Worting, left and Gatwick right).

The Southern used long switches in more locations as the technology developed.

Worting Junction and Gatwick are good examples of this usage. Both required fast crossovers between routes and at Worting the two approaching routes from Southampton and Exeter were both fast and heavily used. From there towards London the fast lines were in the middle of four tracks, requiring the Up Southampton line to cross over from the left hand track to the centre left track. At the same time the turnout to the Up Slow which continues on the left in the first photo (on the same side as Worting Junction Signal Box) did not want to unduly restrict the speed of trains as the nearest station at Basingstoke is still over a mile from these crossovers. So the use of 'F' inclined switches allowed both routes a good speed at this junction and required Up Fast Southampton trains to traverse only one turnout curve when crossing to the central Up Fast line. The Down Side used a long crossover for the Down Fast to Down Southampton route as trains presumably were travelling slightly slower on the rising gradient to the summit at Lichfield Tunnel. Shorter crossovers were then used for the

other movements here, particularly for the rarely used cross-over in the middle between the two Up and two Down lines. Longer crossovers are obviously more expensive and so their usage is restricted to where they are genuinely required.

As with most Permanent Way, the opportunity was considered to upgrade these switches to 'G' switches after these were developed. At the next round of relaying and for many years this was a flagship site in the South as the first real high speed junction (90 mph all lines), though the Southern had already 'pushed' the speed here in previous years with the junction as illustrated here. The new crossovers used the geometry of splitting the turnouts so they had equal radius on each line to maximise the speed through the new layout.

Photo 4, above.

Switches are normally held apart and in the correct position by stretcher bars which in pre-grouping days were usually round. With the advent of REA drawings the new standards contained a number of typical stretcher bars to be used with the new (1926) design S&C, and showed the connection brackets to fit and hold the switch rails.

The minimum number of stretcher bars was, and still is, two, but longer switches have more. The stretcher at the switch tip is the most critical and the points are normally driven or moved by a bracket on this bar.

Often on switches there is a bracket extension to the switch tip which has extra rods attached to each rail for signalling detection. This is so that each switch is constantly checked

at the position it should be relative to the adjacent stock rail. This detection can be electrical and incorporated in contacts in the motor, or mechanical. It is a requirement for switches over which facing moves are made by passenger trains for switches used in the facing direction to be fitted with detection. This photograph shows such an arrangement for a motor-operated exit from a siding to the main line.

Also of note, though not visible, is that the first stretcher bar extends under the stock rail on this switch style, which was an improvement on earlier round types which were simply bolted into the switch rail, sometimes extended through a hole in the stock rail. This extension is specifically to stop the switch 'kicking up' when the weight of a wheel presses on the other end which can lead (and has) to derailments through a flange catching the risen switch and going the wrong side of it.

Photo 5, Page 96 top.

This was taken in 1961 at an unknown Southern Railway site and shows a BH switch diamond (they would be movable elbows if they were on the GWR!). The large crank on the timber end is to ensure the two switches move as opposing switches; they were normally operated from one lever in the signal box. This picture shows the mechanical facing point lock and the two front stretcher bars which have two slots cut after installation on site, through which the shiny parallel lock bar moves in the accurately cut slot for each position. It is pulled out of the slot to allow the switch to move and replaced to prevent any wrong movement after the route has been cleared for a

Photo 7, opposite page.

This shows a catch-point arrangement normally associated with track on a rising gradient to catch any wagons rolling back after a coupling failure. Such arrangements used to exist at Wallers Ash loops north of Winchester, but there were others, as here.

These are shown in the closed position, but normally the left hand switch would be open and spring loaded to remain in that position. The spring would be fitted to the two extended left hand timbers.

Although not obvious from the photo, the two running rails actually went wide to gauge by a measured amount after the two check rails were reached. This caused the wheel flanges to be gradually pushed apart by the effect of the inner check rails, thus slowing by friction only any wheels diverted into the catch point.[3] Sand in narrow channels was sometimes used instead of the wide-to-gauge check rail portion, as an alternative to slow runaway wheels, but the sand tended to get blown away, so the wide-to-gauge arrangement was preferred.

train to pass.

The stock rail is bolted to the slide chairs in the REA design here, but in earlier times such as LSWR days, the nut on the bolt was often replaced with a tapered wedge in a slot in the 'stud bolt.'

Lastly, the pipe-work around the switches is the gas heating for the points, normally powered from nearby bottled gas. This had small burners in the boxes against the web of the rail and would be lit in cold weather.

The system was used for many years and is still in use in some areas. Compared with modern electric heater strips they were low technology, but they worked with only minor problems such as occasionally being blown out by passing trains, though usually the hot glowing gauze inside them was enough to re-ignite them.

Photo 6 - right (Charing Cross).

This shows the approach to Charing Cross during work in 1954, and illustrates that not all point-work is on conventional cross sleepers!

Many small bridges used wheel timber construction for plain track. These are long timbers, running parallel with the rails in general, to spread the load on associated steel cross girders and bearers.

At Charing Cross the flat bridge deck over the Thames allowed some flexibility in the trackwork design, though the actual timbers are fastened to the flat deck by cleats (brackets) and bolts. The use of very large, specially-shaped, timbers spread the load over the girders which are underneath the flat deck-plates. The deck was not strong enough to support a ballasted formation and conventional cross timbers.

Some of these wheel-timbers are truly huge to accommodate the various chairs.

Photo 8, **Page 98.**

Clearly not all turnouts can be straight and this turnout illustrates how standard components would be adapted to fit a curving layout. When both routes in one turnout curve to one side, as here, the turnout is referred to as a similar flexure turnout. When each route diverges in two curves of opposite hand the turnout is called a contra flexure turnout.

The mathematics behind this allows for the radius of standard turnouts to be adapted and quoted for the various different radii normally associated with one turnout, such as switch radius and turnout radius from the switch to the crossing.

The formula for similar flexure being :- $\dfrac{R \times Re}{R + Re} = Rt$

That for contra (opposite) flexure being :- $\dfrac{R \times Re}{R - Re} = Rt$

Where R =Radius of main, Re = Standard turnout radius, Rt = Adapted turnout radius. These apply whatever the style of rail used.

Also of note here are the switch stretcher bars of REA style with three used.

The drive from the motor out of sight on the left is clearly visible to the drive lug attached to this front stretcher. The two front detector bars and connecting bar on the switch

'ears' (extended brackets) are also visible, as is the gas heating.

Note also the check rail extended into the back of the switch as the turnout radius on this passenger route required a continuous check because of its tight radius, this also avoided excessive wear of the left hand turnout rail.

The GW developed check lump switches where the check rail on BH switches extended into the heel fishplated joint of the switches. To achieve this the end of the check rail was machined, along with the end of the closure rail, to reduce the head width to a single rail width and match the end of the switch rail at the heel fishplated joint, thus giving a continuous check rail using the back of the switch itself for the first portion. However the Southern never developed this style of 'checking' and the arrangement shown in the REA designs issued in 1926 was adopted which used an extended check rail which stopped short of the actual switch.

All points are numbered, the number being fitted nearer to the 'Normal' point position. These are clearly 67 points, but the location is not stated. It would appear that the turnout in the foreground is on a falling gradient and the conductor rail stops short of the heel of the switches on both sides and is 'gapped' through the switches. The train would be tending to 'coast' on the downhill gradient and require less current here. On the left, the track is rising and to assist the train to pick up power on the maximum number of shoes, the conductor rail is continuous with a side ramp inside the right hand conductor rail, for shoes continuing on the turnout route.

In many cases the Southern built their structures to the minimum clearance required, often driven by land availability. Then as now, it was important to understand where minimum spaces existed for staff working on the track. Refuges are widely spaced here, and took time to reach!

1. During the First World War the railways were effectively united under the Railway Executive Committee - REC, with engineering matters being handled by the Railway Engineering Association - REA. It was therefore a committee of the REA which produced the Engineering Standards. The committee managed to get most of the parties to agree a common set of standards, but it took from about 1918 to 1924, so it was not an easy matter! These were then published in May 1924. Hence the use of the initials REA, rather than REC, in the accompanying text.

2. P/way, signalling and operations fight over this description to this day, particularly the statement 'in advance of'! Posters were produced by a leading contractor about two years ago to clarify the situation, but even they got it wrong! 'Signalling' usually attempt to say that its perfectly clear to use the terms in advance and in rear, but you would be surprised how many find the term 'in advance' difficult to understand! Conversation then often resorts to army terms, when you advance you go forward. Well at least most armies do! The current term, I believe, is 'on the approach to' but I cannot remember what 'in advance' of has been replaced by! True split switches, with equal diverging radius on each line, are rare as they require special machining of each switch and stock rail.

3. Try to think of being put on a rack, your arms can be pulled apart by the force applied! There comes a physical limit to this, or something has to give!
In the case of wide to gauge trap points the wheels are firmly forced on the axles, so they cant move apart. If the rails they are travelling on, or more importantly the check rails inside these running rails and bolted to them with spacing blocks move apart, then the inside faces of the flanges will grind on the sideface of the check rails at a greater rate as the check rails move apart as the flanges/wheels cant move any further apart. It makes an awful noise and may actually break the check rail chairs, but the friction of the wheels or at least the flanges grinding on the rails will slow very effectively the wheels progress. Its a very small amount of gauge widening, but enough to take up all the slack of the wheelset on the rails over a reasonable length, as long as nothing gives!

COLOUR INTERLUDE

Crawley 1967. A 2Bil set heads a down train as it starts across Brighton Road on its journey southwest – probably to Bognor Regis via Littlehampton. The exit ramp from the down platform is by the fence on the right and on the extreme right is the end of the 'Railway Hotel'. The end of the signal box can just be seen on the left.

Gordon Gravett

Crawley 1966-67. **Opposite top** *- An up train waiting to depart for London Victoria. Regular trains were four or six coaches (mostly six) and were usually made up from 2Bil and 2Hal sets. This is a four car train with a 2Bil set nearest the camera and what appears to be a Bulleid all steel 2HAL set leading.*

Opposite bottom *- The goods yard had been cleared but the goods shed was still standing when this photo was taken in 1966. By then, the only non-passenger traffic was for parcels. The view shows a new canopy that was built over the parcels bay platform in later years.*

This page *- The goods yard was crossed by a long footbridge known locally as 'The Roman Bridge'. By 1966 the yard was closed but on this occasion was occupied by a British Rail Exhibition train. The furthest two coaches appear to be rebuilt from LSWR Iron-clads.*

All by Gordon Gravett - with many thanks also to Gordon for checking the Crawley article and removing the various 'banana skins'.

More than 50 years ago at Three Bridges. Electric loco No. 20003, in its smart green livery with red and white stripe, passing through with what may well be a Newhaven service.

Paul Hersey collection.

THE KEIGHLEY
WORTH VALLE ...WAY
A Guide and History
Martin Bairstow

Published by Martin Bairstow, Fountain Chambers, Halifax, West Yorkshire
Typesetting by Hanson Typesetting Services Ltd., Cross Roads, Keighley, West Yorkshire.
Printed by Appleby & Hardman, Pilsworth Industrial Estate, Bury, Greater Manchester

Introduction

For the first one hundred years of its history the Worth Valley Railway was a very unremarkable institution. It was just one of countless similar branches built in the mid-Victorian period to connect local industry with the nearest main line. It was well engineered (apart from a cheap timber viaduct) but so were most British branch lines.

It functioned for 95 years providing a service for passengers and goods. Then in the early 1960s it joined practically every similar line in the country, falling victim to changing travel patterns aided and abetted by hostile Government policy and a certain lack of imagination on the part of its operators.

What gives the story of the Worth Valley branch a significance out of all proportion to its modest size is the sequence of events which followed the closure in 1962.

When the Preservation Society first declared its intention to acquire and take over the railway, there were sceptics who said that it was impossible to try and turn the clock back. Possibly they were right because the Society never has succeeded in restoring the kind of railway which was operating before 1962. Nor has it ever seriously attempted to do so.

The Keighley & Worth Valley Railway has found a new role quite different from anything which passed before 1962. It is every bit a part of the local economy as ever it used to be. It is certainly as much a part of the national railway network. It is a great deal better known and may well have provided some of the inspiration behind other railway preservation schemes.

The re-opening of the Worth Valley line in 1968 marked the beginning of a second phase of railway preservation. The concept of a volunteer society taking over the operation of a railway had been pioneered by the Talyllyn in 1951 but the Worth Valley was the first line actually to be purchased from British Railways. The re-opening came after six and a half frustrating years during which many similar schemes had fallen by the wayside. After 1968 other projects followed with increasing momentum both at home and abroad.

I joined the Keighley & Worth Valley Railway Preservation Society at the age of 12 in 1964. At that time I was travelling to school by train between Apperley Bridge and Frizinghall Stations both of which were about to succumb to the axe which stood poised over a major part of the railway system. I used to spend all my free time at Apperley Bridge in the booking office or signal box getting up to tricks which would not be permitted today, even on a preserved railway, to anyone below the age of 21. I understand that some Worth Valley members learnt how to fire an engine by doing so 'unofficially' on the main line long before preservation was thought of.

I joined the Society at a meeting at Bradford Grammar School. I think that one of the older pupils was aiming for the 'Rail Rover' ticket being offered to the person who recruited the most new members. The aims of the Society appealed to me greatly. I foresaw running my own railway and putting the Beeching closures into reverse in the process.

Things may not quite have happened exactly or as quickly as then envisaged—especially in my 12 year old mind—but here we are more than 26 years later, able to look back on achievements which have gone beyond the

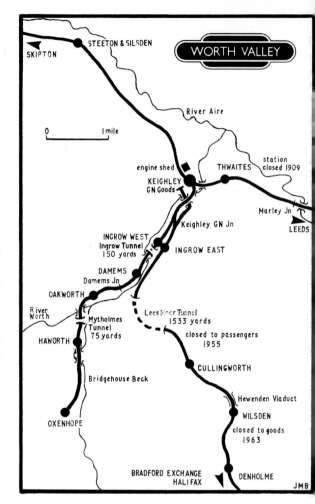

wildest dreams of anybody who was around in the 1960s.

This book is dedicated to the hundreds of Worth Valley volunteers without whom the story would have ended in 1962. So much has already been published about the KWVR, but it is hoped that the present volume does have something new to offer. I am grateful to everybody who has helped in its production.

The photographs are credited individually but special thanks are due to Peter Sunderland, John Halliday and David Mitchell for contributing so much from the pre-closure period. John Holroyd helped with artwork. Geoffrey Lewthwaite advised on tickets. The manuscript was typed by Margaret Jones. Philippa Simpson sampled the various museums and attractions featured in the penultimate chapter. Michael Cope kindly agreed to research and write a short history of the Vintage Carriages Trust. John Sagar, the present editor of Push and Pull! lent his support for the book, with material from his archives.

Thanks also to David Pearson for supplying snippets of historical data.

Halifax, West Yorkshire
January 1991   Martin Bairstow

Early History

The Railway Comes to Keighley . . . .

The 1840s were the years of the 'Railway Mania'—a decade of rapid progress which transformed an embryonic railway system into something very close to a national network.

The Leeds & Bradford Railway was authorised by Parliament in July 1844 to connect the two cities via Shipley. It took just under two years to complete the 13½ miles which included the ¾ mile Thackley Tunnel and the ten arch Apperley Viaduct together with six other bridges over the River Aire and four crossing the Leeds & Liverpool Canal.

Even before its opening on 30 June 1846, the Leeds & Bradford was already well on with its Extension Railway further up the Aire Valley. This had been authorised by an Act of June 1845. Work again proceeded at a rapid pace allowing the line to open from Shipley to Keighley on 16 March 1847 and as far as Skipton on 7 September the same year. Opening through to Colne on 2 October 1848 completed the Leeds & Bradford Extension Railway. A further outlet opened up on 1 June 1850 with completion of the 'Little' North Western Railway from Skipton through to Lancaster and Morecambe.

Both the Leeds & Bradford and the North Western Companies were quickly absorbed into the Midland Railway.

. . . . But not yet to Haworth

There was provision in the Leeds & Bradford Extension Railway Act of 1845 for a number of additional branch lines which were not in fact built. One of these was to have linked Keighley with Haworth.

The Leeds & Bradford would have held every intention of pressing ahead with its Haworth branch—just as soon as other priorities had been dealt with. It was included in the 1845 Bill at least partly to 'buy' the support of influential people in the Worth Valley for the Company's main proposals.

The Haworth branch fell easy prey to the post Railway Mania recession which hit the economy towards the end of the decade.

A much more adventurous, if less probable, scheme for a line through the Worth Valley was the Manchester, Hebden Bridge & Keighley & Leeds & Carlisle Junction Railway. The Reverend Patrick Brontë was amongst the promoters of this enterprise which in 1845 planned a line from Hebden Bridge to Keighley. The rest of the title was just padding to emphasise that the proposed line would have connections at each end.

According to advertisements inviting subscriptions, the estimated cost of the scheme was £350,000 (about £20 million at 1990 prices). This appears hopelessly inadequate, bearing in mind the task of tunnelling under Oxenhope Moor, but the matter was never put to the test as the proposal got nowhere. Even in later years there never was any serious possibility of a railway going beyond Oxenhope to Hebden Bridge.

It was not until the beginning of the 1860s that any real progress was seen towards a railway in the Worth Valley itself.

The Keighley & Worth Valley Railway

John McLandsborough was born in Otley where he practised as a civil engineer more in the field of drains and sewers than of railways. In 1856 his business moved to Bradford but he continued to reside in Otley which, being still without a railway, must have presented a bit of a problem. In the late 1850s he became involved in efforts to try and persuade the Midland Railway to build, or at least support, a line from Bradford to Otley and Ilkley. This objective was achieved and a line opened in 1865.

Meanwhile during 1861, Mr McLandsborough visited Haworth 'as a pilgrim at the shrine of Charlotte Brontë'.

From 1847 until 1883, Keighley Station stood on the Skipton side of what is now the Station bridge. The site became a goods depot then, eventually, Sainsbury's car park.

(Ian Dewhirst collection) **3**

He decided that something ought to be done to improve communications with Haworth and found that his views were shared by a number of influential people in the district.

The main concern of the local mill owners was the difficulty and cost of transporting coal and other raw materials over the relatively short distance from Keighley Station to their premises and the corresponding problem of getting finished goods out. The numerous mills in the Worth Valley were at a considerable disadvantage compared to those in nearby towns and villages already served by rail.

The Midland Railway had no particular reason to be concerned about this. It appeared content to convey goods to and from Keighley Station and let somebody else worry about the local transport problems. It might have been a different story had any other railway company threatened to become involved but in 1860 the Midland had a monopoly over traffic for the Worth Valley. If the road journey from Haworth to Keighley was difficult, to have reached the Great Northern or Lancashire & Yorkshire Railways at Bradford or Halifax would have been impossible.

In these circumstances the standard response of the main line company to requests for a branch line was to invite local interested parties to build it for themselves—with promises of support which in practice often led to the large company eventually taking it over at a discount.

So in October 1861, the Midland Railway told a delegation from the Worth Valley that it would support a Bill for a branch line from Keighley to Oxenhope which it would operate in return for half the receipts.

The local mill owners were not only concerned with the delivery of goods to and from their factories, they also assumed the role of feudal landlords who saw it as part of their responsibility to be involved in improvements to their neighbourhood. They may also have seen the chance of getting a direct return on their investment in a railway in which case they were a little over optimistic.

In the Autumn of 1861, the Keighley & Worth Valley Railway Company was launched with no fewer than 22 provisional directors—most of them drawn from the local mill-owning classes. Only nine of them actually became directors. John McLandsborough was named in the prospectus as 'acting engineer'. The superior position of 'consulting engineer' was afforded to J S Crossley of the Midland Railway, but that was just protocol.

The Keighley & Worth Valley Railway Bill became an Act on 30 June 1862. The required capital was subscribed by about 200 individuals. In November 1863, the contract to build the line was awarded to John Metcalfe of Bradford. On Shrove Tuesday, 9 February 1864, the ceremony of cutting the first sod was performed by the Chairman of the Company, Sir Isaac Holden. That ritual over, attention at last could be turned to the real business in hand.

Less than a year earlier, on 10 March 1863, Sir Isaac Holden had also officiated when the foundation stone was laid for a new Wesley Place Methodist Chapel at Ingrow. This stood above the railway which was to go under Halifax Road by means of a 150 yard tunnel at the

For the first 25 years, the railway crossed the Vale Mill Dam South of Oakworth by a timber viaduct. It was bypassed in 1892 when Mytholmes Viaduct and Tunnel were completed. The loco appears to be a Kirtley 0-6-0 Well tank.

exit from Ingrow Station.

As work proceeded on the tunnel, a layer of wet sandy soil was pierced. The immediate problem was overcome by driving in piles until they reached solid rock. Unfortunately the combination of vibration and subsidence caused extensive damage to the Chapel which had to be rebuilt further back. Quite naturally the Trustees claimed compensation from the Railway Company. The matter went to arbitration, damages of just under £2,000 being awarded. This sum represents over £100,000 at 1990 values, but it is perhaps more meaningful to relate it to the £36,000 estimated cost of building the railway. This was just one factor which caused the eventual cost to reach three times that figure.

The line also took three times as long to complete as the one year which had been estimated. It is part of local folklore that a cow ate the plans left in a field whilst surveyors partook of lunch. A more serious and more credible source of delay was the alleged failure of the contractor to employ sufficient labour to do the job. The Company attempted to 'fine' him for late completion.

By the Autumn of 1866, the railway was nearing completion. The contractor was able to borrow an engine on 1 November and run a train from Keighley to Oxenhope and back for the benefit of Mr McLandsborough and the Keighley Station Master along with some of their respective staff, who travelled in an open wagon fitted with 'ad hoc' seating.

It was hoped that the line would soon be open but on 14 November disaster struck. This part of the country suffered severe storms that day. Damage to the railways included the collapse of Apperley Viaduct between Leeds and Shipley. On the Worth Valley line forty yards of embankment were washed away near Damems leaving the track suspended over the gap. There was also minor damage elsewhere causing a delay of some five months in completing the railway.

The Railway is opened

Outstanding work was finished and the opening date fixed for Saturday 13 April 1867. The first train, conveying invited guests, comprised a tank engine, seven coaches and a guards van. It was a dull drizzling day. The rails were wet and the train slipped to a halt on the 1 in 58 gradient outside Keighley—an embarrassment which has recurred many times since. The train set back for another attempt and this time it was successful in getting clear of Keighley but it stopped between Oakworth and Haworth and had to complete the journey in two sections. The guests then repaired to the Mechanics Institute in Haworth for a celebratory dinner. Even that was a last minute improvisation because planned arrangements at the Black Bull had been cancelled the previous afternoon. Whilst the dignatories were preparing to 'tuck in' members of the general public were taking their first trips over the new railway.

Normal passenger service commenced the following Monday 15 April but goods traffic was not handled until 1 July. The contractor remained responsible for maintaining the branch for twelve months then the Midland Railway took over that function.

On 25 May 1867, just six weeks after the opening, the Keighley News commented favourably on the contribution which the Railway was already making.

A view across the future site of the 1883 station showing the Worth Valley branch coming in from the left to join the main line from Leeds. The train is passing through what became platform 2. The age of the photograph must excuse the quality. Just visible is the 'lofty' signal cabin controlling Worth Valley Junction. *(Ian Dewhirst collection)*

Looking down from Keighley water tower in 1959. 41273 is ready to leave for Oxenhope. It appears as though platform 3 had already lost two canopy arches.   *J. C. W. Halliday*

3F No. 43586 has taken the branch goods to the far end of the goods yard by Keighley North Box. Opposite a sister locomotive stands outside Keighley Engine Shed.
(Peter Sunderland

"Since the Worth Valley Railway was opened it has been the means already of bringing thousands of visitors to the ancient village of Haworth. During the past few Sundays, hundreds have been seen enjoying the pure air and mountain breezes in the romantic neighbourhood. To all appearances it is very likely to become a general pleasure locality in the summer months."

The arrangement by which the Midland Railway operated the branch lasted until 1 July 1881 when the main line company took over complete control. The Keighley & Worth Valley Company remained in existance for a further five years drawing an annual ground rent until it was dissolved under the Midland Railway Act of 1886.

The local Company appears to have spent most of its existence in dispute with the Midland Railway. The balance sheet at 30 June 1881 revealed a sum of nearly £10,000 (worth over £½m in 1990) owing from the Midland, representing sundry items in dispute between the two companies.

At an Extraordinary General Meeting held on 22 August 1885, it was admitted that the branch, 'whilst being an immense advantage to the Worth Valley had not been very profitable for individual shareholders'. The KWVR company derived no financial recompense for the benefit accruing to the Midland Railway from the additional main line traffic brought about by goods and passengers travelling to and from the branch line. The Worth Valley Railway was a great deal more successful than would appear from the rather disappointing dividends paid to its shareholders. The Midland Railway could treat the local Company more or less as it liked, settling accounts as when and if it pleased.

New Works at Keighley

The take over of the branch had become necessary in 1881 because the Midland was obliged to spend money on the Worth Valley line in order to accommodate the Great Northern Railway at Keighley. This Company was building its heavily engineered route from Halifax and Bradford via Queensbury and required a junction with the Keighley & Worth Valley Railway. Had the Midland not acted both to gain ownership of the branch and to make provision for Great Northern traffic then there was a possibility that the latter Company might have attempted to take over the Worth Valley line presumably diverting trains to an independent passenger station near to what became the GNR goods depot.

This didn't happen. Instead the Midland provided a new station at Keighley and doubled the first ¾ mile of the Worth Valley line as far as what became Keighley GN Junction.

The original Keighley Station was on the Skipton side of the Bradford Road level crossing which in 1879 was replaced by the Station Bridge. The new station, which opened on 6 May 1883, was built on the opposite side of the road, a fraction nearer to Leeds.

It had two platforms on the main line plus a bay and two more curving off at an angle for the Worth Valley and future GNR trains. Access was from the station bridge and the main offices were at road level. Ramps led down to the platforms which were also linked by a subway. The additional platform on the Leeds bound side was not numbered but known as 'the bay line'. It has only been filled in and landscaped comparatively recently.

The old station was demolished to make way for an

A view across Ingrow Goods Yard about 1900 with a variety of wagons belonging to collieries, to local firms and to the Midland Railway.

Ian Dewhirst collection)

7

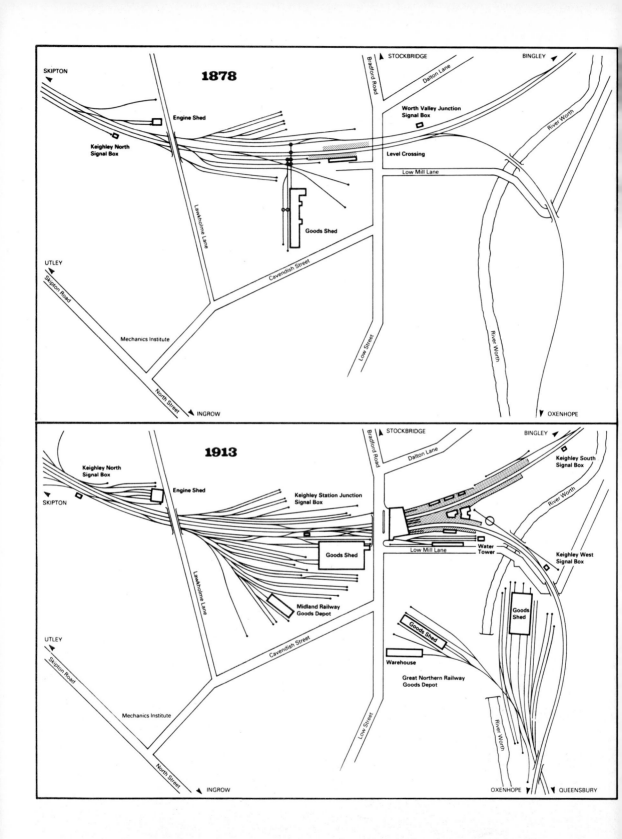

The layout at Keighley Station before and after the changes of 1883.

2-6-4T No. 42052 waiting to leave Keighley with the 1.15pm for Oxenhope in June 1957. This lunchtime working (Mondays to Fridays) was not push-pull. *(Peter Sunderland)*

Most Worth Valley passenger trains were push-pull operated from the 1930s. The locomotive was invariably at the Oxenhope end. This train arriving at Keighley in 1952 is being driven from the leading coach. *(D. Ibbotson)*

expansion of the goods yard. The site is now Sainsburys car park.

As built, the line had climbed out of Keighley by means of a 13 arch stone and iron viaduct upwards of 150 yards in length. When the track was doubled, this was obliterated in favour of the substantial stone supported embankment which carries the line above the site of the GNR Goods Yard.

Improvements elsewhere on the branch

After leaving Oakworth Station towards Haworth, the original line crossed the Vale Mill Dam by a timber trestle viaduct. There were a number of other lines where this method of construction had been adopted, presumably on the grounds of economy. There was a speed restriction over the viaduct which was considered to have only a limited life. In June 1891 work started on a deviation nearly half a mile in length involving a three arch viaduct, four other bridges and the 75 yard Mytholmes Tunnel.

On Sunday 6 November 1892, the 7.25 am train for Oxenhope passed over the old viaduct. Then the permanent way was reconnected at each end of the deviation to allow the 10.50 am for Keighley to pass through the new tunnel.

When the railway was built, sufficient land had been purchased for double track and all bridges, including those on the 1892 deviation, were built wide enough to accommodate a second line at a later date. This never happened

other than between Keighley and GN Junction.

However the capacity of the line was increased from 4 April 1900 when the branch was divided into three block sections with passing loops at Oakworth and Haworth controlled by a better signalling system described later.

The platform at Haworth was lengthened about the turn of the century by a wooden extension which is still evident today. Some time later the level crossing at the Oxenhope end of the platform was replaced by the footbridge which links the station with the village.

The 1875 Runaway

Present day Worth Valley staff are well aware of the ease with which vehicles could start moving downhill especially on wet or greasy rails if not properly secured. If there are any doubts on the subject then they need only consider what nearly happened to porter John Wigglesworth on the morning of 27 September 1875.

At that time, Keighley Station was in its old position and the branch began at Worth Valley Junction on the Leeds side of the level crossing. The branch was operated as one single line section with a staff. There was no telegraph and the telephone hadn't even been invented. As a safety (or damage limitation) measure, there was a catch point at Ingrow. This was set after the passage of an Oxenhope train in order to derail any loose wagons which might decide to come back but it was reset to the normal position to allow passage of a legiti-

It was from here that the runaway started. Oakworth Yard in December 1955 with the passing loop and home signal still in position.
(Peter Sunderland)

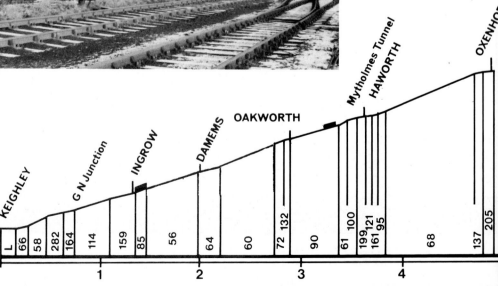

mate train towards Keighley.

At 6.13 am a train left Keighley comprising a tank engine, six goods vehicles, five coal wagons, a brake van, five empty passenger coaches and another brake van. The passenger coaches were to work the first departure from Oxenhope. There were four crew; driver Benjamin Whitfield, the fireman, guard Abraham Welch and Keighley porter John Wigglesworth who was in charge of the passenger stock.

After dropping a wagon at Ingrow, the train drew to a stand by Oakworth goods yard where the wagon nearest the engine was to be deposited. Guard Welch instructed Wigglesworth to screw down the hand brake in the rear van whilst he himself applied one other hand brake. He ignored the rule which required all vehicles left on the main line to be handbraked and spragged. A sprag was a piece of wood placed between the spokes of the wheel. Welch uncoupled the front wagon and rode on it as the loco shunted it into the yard.

Suddenly Welch noticed that the rest of his train had started to move. He leapt off, ran to the train and attempted to throw a sprag into one of the wheels but it missed. He then climbed on the engine which set off in pursuit of the runaways.

Meanwhile Wigglesworth had rather courageously climbed into his van, whilst on the move, and tried to screw the hand brake down harder but to no avail. The train gathered momentum. The rest of the helpless crew followed on the engine making liberal use of the whistle.

The train should have been derailed at Ingrow but porter Jeremiah Laycock, in charge of that station, heard the whistling which he interpreted as a signal that a normal train was coming from Oxenhope. He set the catch point to let it go through to Keighley. He could not, of course, see what was coming because of Ingrow Tunnel.

The runaway continued towards Keighley with the engine in pursuit. Apparently the driver, fireman and guard considered, when they had almost caught it up, whether one of them could clamber over the coal bunker and try to reach the coupling. They decided against it.

At Keighley, a Bradford to Colne passenger train had just come to a stand in the station when the signalman at Worth Valley Junction saw what was coming down the branch. His shouts and the repeated whistling combined to alert the station staff who hurriedly persuaded a number of passengers to leave the train then told the driver to depart. Unfortunately he had stopped the engine on 'dead centre' and required two abortive attempts at starting before he set back a little then began to go forward. The Colne train was barely on the move when the collision happened.

Fourteen passengers received fairly minor injuries but John Wigglesworth secured a very lucky escape. From his vantage point in the leading compartment he would have had an unobscured view of the line ahead and of his impending doom. Just before the crash he fell to the floor. He was unconscious for a brief time but came round unhurt. His van had gone under the rear coach of the Colne train forcing that up through the platform awning.

The outcome could have been a great deal worse. The electric telegraph was introduced in 1877 and guard Abraham Welch appears to have kept his job.

Midland 3F 0-6-0 No 3337 on Keighley Turntable during the 1930s.

(Jack Adams, courtesy Terry Sykes)

The Great Northern goods depot used to occupy a large site inside the curve by which Worth Valley trains pull out of Keighley. The main goods shed is now a depot for Yorkshire Electricity. *J. C. W. Halliday)*

A dmu descending from GN Junction towards Keighley in 1960. The tunnel on the right is on the GN goods line. *(Peter Sunderland)*

Train Services 1867–1962

When the Worth Valley branch first opened, there were six trains daily each way on weekdays but only two on Sundays. After six months the timetable had been modified slightly and the following is the entry in Bradshaw for October 1867. By this time the tiny station at Damems had opened.

	WEEKDAYS					S.O.		SUNDAYS		
	A.M.	P.M.	P.M.	P.M.	P.M.	P.M.	A.M.	A.M.	P.M.	P.M.
ighley	8.35	12.20	2.20	5.00	6.40	8.30	7.50	10.40	2.05	7.20
row	8.41	12.26	2.26	5.06	6.45	8.36	7.56	10.46	2.11	7.26
mems	8.44	–	–	–	6.48	–	–	–	–	–
kworth	8.47	12.32	2.32	5.12	6.50	8.42	8.02	10.52	2.17	7.32
worth	8.53	12.38	2.38	5.18	6.54	8.48	8.08	10.58	2.23	7.38
enhope	9.00	12.45	2.45	5.25	7.00	8.55	8.15	11.05	2.30	7.45

	WEEKDAYS						SUNDAYS			
	A.M.	A.M.	P.M.	P.M.	P.M.	P.M	A.M.	P.M.	P.M.	P.M.
enhope	8.00	9.20	1.30	3.50	5.50	7.10	8.30	12.55	6.30	8.00
worth	8.06	9.26	1.36	3.56	5.56	7.14	8.36	1.01	6.36	8.06
kworth	8.12	9.32	1.42	4.02	6.02	7.18	8.42	1.07	6.42	8.12
mems	8.15	–	–	–	6.05	–				
row	8.18	9.38	1.48	4.08	6.08	7.23	8.48	1.13	6.48	8.18
ghley	8.25	9.45	1.55	4.15	6.15	7.30	8.55	1.20	6.55	8.25

). - SATURDAYS ONLY

The practice of starting the first train at Oxenhope was logical enough from the traffic point of view but it necessitated running an empty train up the branch first thing in the morning. In the early years this was achieved by attaching the passenger stock to a goods train as on the occasion of the 1875 runaway.

By 1880 the number of trains had risen to eight on weekdays and five on Sundays. There was an increasing trade in early morning workmen who from 1883 were entitled by statute to travel at lower fares provided that their outward journey was completed before 8 am.

The absence before 1900 of intermediate passing loops forced some goods traffic to move at night. The 1898 working timetable shows an engine leaving Keighley Shed at 2.35am to work a 2.50 return trip to Ingrow followed by a 3.50 all stations (or yards) to Oxenhope.

By the early years of the twentieth century, the service had doubled again in frequency with 16 departures from Keighley on Monday to Saturday with two extras on Saturday and a Sunday service of seven trains. The first trains were as early as 5.07 am from Oxenhope and 5.25 am from Keighley. These must have been separate trains. In both the morning and tea time peaks there were two passenger trains on the branch at the same time but, unless they were scheduled to pass between Keighley and GN Junction, one of them always ran empty. The loops at Oakworth and Haworth were not intended to pass two passenger trains. It was the movement of goods which had benefitted most from the signalling improvements in 1900. With a passenger train somewhere on the branch almost all the time, the pick up goods could move fairly freely between Keighley, Oakworth and Haworth taking whatever time was necessary to shunt these yards. It would have to get from Haworth to Oxenhope and back between passenger trains and would also have to be careful how long it occupied the Oakworth to GN Junction section in the course of shunting Damems, Clough's Mill and Ingrow Yard.

The timetable for Summer 1938 shows the best passenger service ever enjoyed by the Worth Valley branch with departures as follows:

From Keighley	From Oxenhope
6.09 am	5.49 am
7.20	6.35
8.17	7.05
9.12	7.41
11.20	8.40
12.23 pm SO	9.39
1.10	10.48
1.50	11.40
2.55 SO	12.47 pm SO
4.16	1.35
4.56	2.15
5.43	3.22 SO
6.04	3.56
6.50	4.35
7.55	5.17
8.55	6.26
9.42	7.30
10.46	8.19
11.30	9.22
	10.10
	11.10

SUNDAY

From Keighley

7.00 am
11.25
1.55 pm
6.10
7.35
9.05

From Oxenhope

7.27 am
12.25 pm
2.45
6.30
8.00
9.25

Haworth booking office was manned up to its last day on 30 December 1961. *(John Holroyd)*

The Worth Valley side of Keighley Station used to be shared with services to Bradford and Halifax via Queensbury. Great Northern class N1 0-6-2T No. 69471 awaits departure from platform 3 shortly before withdrawal of the service in May 1955. *(Peter Sunderland)*

An LNER B1 4-6-0 and a Great Northern 0-6-0 dropping down to Keighley in July 1955 with excursion stock from one of the sidings on the GN line, probably Cullingworth, which they are going to work back over the GN line to Cleethorpes. *(Peter Sunderland)*

The 4.50pm Keighley to Halifax leaving the Worth Valley line at GN Junction behind N1 0-6-2T No. 69436 on 30 April 1955. *(Peter Sunderland)*

Journey times were about 16 minutes or 17 on the minority of trains which stopped at Damems. The 11.10 pm from Oxenhope was advertised to run non-stop in ten minutes. This was the only train to miss intermediate stations other than Damems. Push-Pull operation allowed turn round times to be reduced to three minutes. Again it can be calculated from the timetable that there were empty stock trains passing the advertised service at either Oakworth or Haworth.

The Second World War imposed cuts which were never fully restored. In 1948, the first year of British Railways, there were nine trains each way, Monday to Fridays. There were 12 on Saturdays but the Sunday service had finished permanently in 1947. There were still trains in the early morning at 6.11, 6.50 and 8.00 from Keighley but then there were long gaps with nothing until 1.15 pm and a further interval until 4.05. About half the trains still called at Damems until it closed in May 1949.

With this standard of service and only a daily pick up goods, there was no need for the loops and signal boxes at Oakworth and Haworth. These were dispensed with early in 1956.

About the same time a three coach gangwayed push-pull set was introduced so that the guard could issue the tickets at branch stations. Ingrow and Oxenhope became unstaffed, Oakworth was staffed for the level crossing and there was a station master for the entire branch based at Haworth.

In July 1959 BR announced its intention to close the branch. To do this they needed the agreement of the Transport Users Consultative Committee. This body met to consider the matter on 1 September 1959. Also on the agenda that day was an application by BR to

Excursion opportunities from Worth Valley Stations in 1931.
(David Beeken collection)

The driver of an Oxenhope to Keighley push-pull has just passed the token to the signalman at GN Junction in July 1955.
(Peter Sunderland)

withdraw passenger services from the Holmfirth branch. Keighley Corporation presented quite a coherent case against closure, a point commented on favourably at a subsequent meeting of the Holmfirth Urban District Council because they had failed miserably. The TUCC had recommended in favour of closing the Holmfirth branch but urged BR to try and develop the Worth Valley line.

The Worth Valley had been excluded from the general dieselisation which had affected local services in Airedale and Wharfedale from January 1959. However from 12 June 1960, an enhanced service of diesel multiple units was introduced giving 15 return trips between Keighley and Oxenhope Mondays to Fridays and no fewer than 20 on Saturdays. There were only 19 one way because the last train at 11.15 pm from Keighley came back empty. There was still no Sunday service.

The only major gap in the frequency was mid-morning when the dmu retreated to allow the branch goods to do its work.

Unfortunately it was not long before BR returned to the TUCC renewing the request for closure saying that the improvements had failed to generate sufficient additional revenue. This time they were successful and in October 1961 notices were posted saying that the passenger service would end on Saturday 30 December with goods traffic continuing just a further six months.

The last day saw quite a heavy snowfall. Most trains were worked by a four car set. About 150 people joined the 11.15 pm departure from Keighley which on this occasion returned as a passenger working. So ended almost 95 years of service. The pick up goods pottered on for a few more months.

The TUCC procedure described above was before the 1962 Transport Act when the Committee was much nearer to fulfilling the role of a Tribunal. Sometimes they found in favour of BR, sometimes the other way. Closures, at that time, did not excite that much interest but if the local authority objected on behalf of travellers there was a reasonable chance of at least temporary success.

When Transport Minister Ernest Marples came to introduce Dr. Beeching in 1961, it was clear to him that the prevailing TUCC procedure would frustrate any mass closure plans. Therefore the system was changed under the 1962 Act so that the TUCC merely reported its findings on the one subject of hardship to the Minister of Transport who himself made the decision with or without regard to those findings.

The 1962 Act is still in operation but there have been very few closures since the early 1970s. Nowadays the TUCC fills in time by advertising for people to make complaints over BR services.

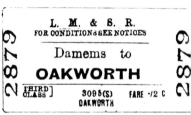

Ingrow Station and Tunnel in September 1955. It became unstaffed in March 1958. It was described as 'neat but somewhat small' by the *Keighley News* in its report on the Opening in 1867.   *(A. M. Ross)*

44055 passing Ingrow with a freight early in 1962. The old station building was less impressive and less like the others on the branch than its present day replacement. *(D. J. Mitchell)*

Emerging from Ingrow Tunnel in April 1956. The hut on the right houses the ground frame for Clough's siding. *(Peter Sunderland)*

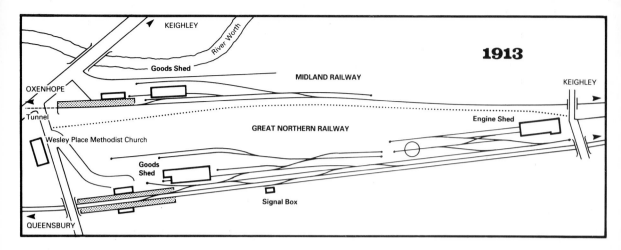

1913

KEIGHLEY

River Worth

Goods Shed

MIDLAND RAILWAY

KEIGHLEY

OXENHOPE

Engine Shed

Tunnel

GREAT NORTHERN RAILWAY

Wesley Place Methodist Church

Goods
Shed

Signal Box

QUEENSBURY

The two adjacent stations at Ingrow.

The classic view of Damems and staff in Midland days. Opened 1 September 1867 and closed 21 May 1949.
Damems once boasted a siding. By the 1930s it saw little traffic other than milk. *(Robin Higgins collection)*

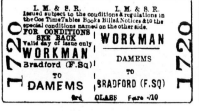

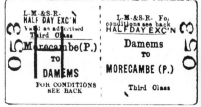

18

Ivatt 2-6-2T No. 41325 passing Damems on 27 April 1957   *(J. C. W. Halliday)*

Oakworth Station in the summer of 1955 when the signal box and passing loop were still in operation.
(Peter Sunderland)

The staff at Oakworth Station pose for the camera about 1904.
(Peter E. Baughan collection)

Mytholmes Tunnel, 75 yards, looking towards Oakworth. The inscription on the stone work reads 'MR 1892'. Clearly double track was held out as a future prospect. *(D. Ibbotson)*

3F 0-6-0 No 43586 has three wagons of coal for Haworth in October 1961. It has just left Mytholmes Tunnel and negotiated the curve which leads off the 1892 deviation back onto the original alignment.
(Peter Sunderland)

The three arch viaduct at Mytholmes on the 1892 deviation which avoided the timber structure across the Vale Mill Dam. 44055 approaches with the pick up goods. *(D. J. Mitchell)*

41325 approaching Mytholmes Tunnel with a two coach push-pull set for Oxenhope in July 1955.
(Peter Sunderland)

41273 approaching Haworth with a strengthened train on Keighley Gala Day 1957. The Preservation Society normally runs additional trains on Keighley Gala Day including in the late evening.
(Peter Sunderland)

Haworth Station in original form. At that time the goods shed was similar in size to others on the branch. Later a much larger one was provided.
(Robin Higgins collection)

HAWORTH STATION, M.R.

About the turn of the century, the station was enlarged and a new footbridge provided.
(Peter E. Baughan collection)

41273 passing Haworth Signal Box in April 1956. The box had closed the previous month. The Bridgehouse Beck was diverted during construction of the Railway so as to avoid it crossing several times near this point. *(Peter Sunderland)*

2-6-4T No 42052 running round the lunch time train at Oxenhope in June 1957. The push-pull set did not work this particular service. The headshunt was too short for some tender locomotives until the Preservation Society extended it. *(Peter Sunderland)*

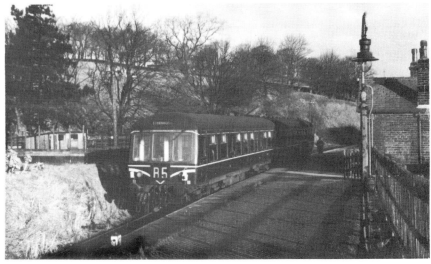

The diesels gave travellers a much better view of the line. The nearest compartment in the trailer car (nearest) was first class but the branch service was advertised as second class only. You could probably use it with impunity.

(D.J. Mitchell)

Oxenhope became unstaffed in December 1955. The building was normally locked and passengers entered by the side gate. 41273 has arrived with a push-pull set in 1959.
(J.C.W. Halliday)

The slightly run down branch terminus in April 1957. In the foreground is the weighbridge at the entrance to the goods yard.
(J.C.W. Halliday)

The Final Day of Passenger Service

Saturday, 30 December 1961
saw a few inches of snow.
A handful of passengers alight at
Ingrow from an Oxenhope
bound train.

(John Holroyd)

Passing Oakworth on the last day.
(J.C.W. Halliday)

Leaving Haworth for Oxenhope.
The diesel service had only
lasted 18 months.
(Peter Sunderland)

There were 20 trains each way on Saturdays. The turn round times at Oxenhope were generally short.

(J.C.W. Halliday)

11.40pm. The Mayor of Keighley prepares to join the final departure from Oxenhope.

(Peter Sunderland)

The Last Special

Midland 3F 0-6-0 No 43586, sporting express train headcodes, storms out of Keighley with the last BR train over the Worth Valley branch on 23 June 1962.

(Peter Sunderland)

Passing Damems. A ten minute booked stop at Ingrow had allowed the photographer to overtake the train. No 43586 was scrapped later in 1962.
(Peter Sunderland)

Just a week after the last train had gone, the rot appears to be setting in at Haworth.
(Peter E. Baughan)

The station forecourt had become a free car park for the Conservative Club. The fading posters include the closure notice, and excursion to Morecambe and car park charges for BR customers.
(Peter E. Baughan)

Would Oxenhope ever see another train?
(Peter E. Baughan)

Six and a Half Frustrating Years

Haworth Station forecourt in May 1965. Vice-Chairman Edgar Chapman promotes a 'win a car' competition in aid of the struggling society. You had to guess how far it would go on one gallon of petrol. The venture just managed to make a profit.
(Geoffrey Lewthwaite)

The Worth Valley branch had been carrying around 130,000 passengers in its final years. Many of these were the same people travelling every day. No doubt some of them grumbled at the enforced change in their travelling habits but they quickly adapted to using the very frequent bus services. In time many people deserted the buses in favour of their own cars, or possibly retired to make way for a new generation for whom a car is the very essence of life.

There the story of the Worth Valley Railway might have ended had there not been one or two pairs of eyes focussed on the impending closure and thinking in terms of an alternative future.

Ralph Povey lived in Oakworth and worked in Bradford. Because of the distance from Oakworth Station he travelled by bus to Keighley thence by train to Bradford. Ralph had followed the fortunes of the early railway preservation schemes. As early as September 1959, he had a letter published in *Trains Illustrated* calling for a 'National Federation of Railway Preservation Societies' to 'direct the limited available finance, volunteer labour and technical advice into channels where it could do most good'.

During November 1961, when the Worth Valley passenger service had just a few weeks still to run, Ralph wrote a letter to the Bradford *Telegraph & Argus* suggesting that a preservation society be formed to take over the branch.

Meanwhile Bob Cryer had also been writing to the local press. In 1960, his cause was a call for the restoration of passenger services over the ex Great Northern line from Keighley to Bradford. At the time the GN route was completely disused between Ingrow and Cullingworth and was rapidly deteriorating along the rest of its length. Bob's campaign met with no success but the demise of the GN line determined him that the nearby Worth Valley branch should not suffer the same fate — if he could do anything to prevent it. So, on Wednesday 24 January 1962 — just 3½ weeks after the passenger closure — a public meeting was called at the Temperance Hall, Keighley. The attendance was most encouraging.

A Committee was delegated to explore the possibilities. This body met on 8 February to consider progress so far. It was reported that some local businesses were in favour of keeping the line open. British Railways had been approached and had not rejected out of hand the idea that they might dispose of the branch to a new operator. Preliminary discussions had been held with the owners of a privately preserved locomotive and a set of coaches. In view of this apparent progress, it was resolved to advertise a further public meeting at the Temperance Hall on Thursday 1 March at which a preservation society would be formed.

If Ralph Povey and Bob Cryer share the honour of having created the idea, there were others not far behind them. The meeting on 1 March was again well attended and the resolution was duly passed bringing the Keighley & Worth Valley Railway Preservation Society into being.

The Society's objective was to take over the branch and to re-introduce passenger services between Keighley and Oxenhope. It was envisaged that a lease would be negotiated with British Railways and that, hopefully, this would be achieved quickly so that the freight service could be kept going. A small staff would be employed to handle this together with a weekday passenger service but members of the Society working on a voluntary basis would provide a steam service at weekends.

An obvious first step was for the Society to charter a special train. This would boost morale, attract publicity and, if all else failed, give people a last chance to travel over the branch. So, on Saturday 23 June, a six coach train was hauled from Bradford Forster Square to Oxenhope and back by a locomotive which had been very familiar on the branch goods — 3F 0-6-0 No 43586. The event was a success but, if it was intended to signify the beginning of a new era, it actually served to mark the end of the old one. It was a full six years before the next public train.

Withdrawal of the freight service had taken place, as planned, on the weekend prior to the special train. After that the track was no longer maintained so BR would not permit any further charter operations.

The Society offered to lease the line following the precedent set by the Bluebell Railway. This idea was dismissed by BR who insisted that negotiations could continue only on the basis of the branch being sold. In June 1962, BR also turned down an offer to purchase the line by means of deferred payments spread over a number of years, insisting on outright sale at a figure of £34,000 for the 4 miles from GN Junction to Oxenhope.

Some local businesses had expressed interest in using the railway once it reopened but when they were approached for assistance—either to subscribe capital or to guarantee a commercial loan—they didn't want to know. Keighley Corporation, which had opposed closure of the railway, also showed a distinct lack of interest when invited to participate in its reopening.

The idea of a public share issue was considered. Basically well wishers and philanthropists would have been invited to purchase shares in a public company with no hope of a return on their investment other than free tickets and the satisfaction of a job well done. This idea has been practised many times since with mixed results. Nobody knew then whether it could succeed. Another idea was to try and seek out one person or perhaps a handful of individuals with an interest in railways and sufficient surplus wealth to back the scheme for personal enjoyment. The Society may have had in mind the character played by Stanley Holloway in *The Titfield Thunderbolt* who had been enticed into filling such a role by the knowledge that there was no restriction on the hours during which rail passengers on the move could be served alcoholic refreshments.

We will never know whether such a benefactor could have been found. The Society was wary of the idea, for-seeing difficulties in reconciling the interests of the proprietor(s) and the volunteer workers—unless they were the same people.

At the end of 1962, there were 266 members of the Preservation Society, but the lack of progress caused this to fall to a low of 140 by March 1964. It was a vicious circle. More members were required if the Society was to succeed but more would not join unless there was some sign of progress.

Everybody knew that there were physical, financial and practical problems to be faced but these could not even start to be tackled until the Society had overcome two far greater hurdles. The first of these was to persuade anybody to take its proposals seriously and the second was to overcome 'official' opposition to its plans.

In August 1963 BR threatened to begin recovering the track unless the Society put forward a firm proposal to purchase the line. At a meeting with BR in York on 4 October 1963 things at last began to look up. The Society offered to purchase the line by means of payments spread over 49 years. BR shortened the period to 25 years but otherwise agreed to sell the line from GN Junction to Oxenhope on this basis for £34,000 + interest. It then took several months for this agreement to be ratified by the BR Board. At last in September 1964, the Society felt able to inform the press that the way was clear towards reopening and that services would hopefully resume at Whitsuntide 1965.

That target date proved to be out by some three years and one month. There were just a few more frustrating obstacles still to be overcome. Morale received a considerable boost from January 1965 when locomotives and coaches began to arrive. In anticipation of this, the

Class N2 0-6-2T No. 4744 at Ingrow on 31 July 1965 with six newly arrived carriages including the three Metropolitan vehicles now owned by the VCT. The locomotive is now based at Loughborough on the Great Central Railway.   *(W. H. Foster Courtesy John Holroyd)*

Society had been given permission to maintain the track. Another small milestone was the first issue in February 1965 of *Push and Pull*, a quarterly magazine for members.

It took until January 1966 for the detailed terms of sale to be agreed between the Society and BR. So far only the route south of GN Junction was involved because one track had remained in use between that point and Keighley for the benefit of an occasional coal train to the former GNR goods yard at Ingrow East. It had been envisaged that the Worth Valley would pay rent for its trains to use the second track into Keighley Station, probably with no run round facility there.

At the height of the Beeching period small goods yards were being swept away even faster than passenger facilities. Scarcely could a railway closure have been more welcome than when the last coal train ran to Ingrow East in June 1965. BR advised the Society of its willingness to include the additional ¾ mile in the sale and it only took until April 1966 to agree a new price of £45,000 for the entire line. Unfortunately there was then a delay until December 1966 waiting for BR Board approval because they couldn't decide on the precise boundary of the land to be sold at Keighley.

As finally agreed the sale comprised the land, buildings and track from just outside Keighley Station to Oxenhope. Payment was by equal six monthly instalments over 25 years with interest. Platform 4 at Keighley was to be leased over the same 25 year period.

This agreement removed the need to raise large amounts of capital. In February 1966 a company called Keighley & Worth Valley Light Railway Ltd was incorporated with an authorised share capital of £10,000. A few individuals bought shares but the majority were taken up by the Society out of its subscription income, retail sales and general fund raising. Control of the operating company has thus always remained firmly in the hands of the Society.

The next stage in the slow process towards reopening was for the KWVR Company to take over statutory authority to operate the line. Almost all railways were built under private Acts of Parliament and normally a private Bill would be required to transfer a line from one body to another. But in 1896 the Government had introduced the Light Railways Act in an attempt to facilitate the construction of new lines in rural areas. A Light Railway is not defined in the Act but 'low speed' would be a good description.

Comparatively few lines were built under this legislation but it has proved popular in more recent times with preservation schemes because it avoids the need for a private Act of Parliament. Instead a Light Railway Order can be issued by the Department of Transport.

Two orders were required. The first brought the branch within the Light Railway legislation but still under BR control. Then a Transfer Order assigned the power to operate the Railway to its new owners. Both orders had to be advertised and a period allowed for objections. The local bus company, 50% owned by Keighley Corporation, objected that the railway might threaten the public interest if it imposed on their monopoly. They were bought off with an agreement not to undercut the bus fares.

Keighley Corporation itself got into its head the idea that the ratepayers might be saddled with a tremendous liability over bridges once BR withdrew from the scene. The Railway Company was obliged to sign an agreement promising to hand over all its assets to the Corporation in the event of failure of the enterprise.

The British Railways (Keighley & Worth Valley) Light Railway Order came into force in October 1967 to be followed by the Transfer Order on 27 May 1968. It only remained for the line to be inspected by Colonel Robertson of the Department of Transport who, on Saturday 8 June, expressed himself satisfied.

At 2.35 pm on Saturday 29 June the aspirations of Society members were finally realised when Ivatt 2-6-2T No 41241 and USA 0-6-0T No 30072 double headed the reopening special out of Keighley Station non stop to Oxenhope.

The sums of money mentioned in this chapter must be multiplied by a factor of about 10 to arrive at their 1990 value in terms of purchasing power.

41241 and 30072 were in charge of the Re-opening Special on 29 June 1968. The same combination is seen with Pullman Cars 'Zena' and No 84 (now 'Mary') at Haworth a few weeks later.
(Martin Bairstow collection)

Customers approach the Worth Valley departure platform by the ramp leading down from the Station Bridge.
(John Bateman)

According to passenger surveys, 'a significant minority', perhaps as many as 20% of Worth Valley customers arrive by connecting train. We will assume that most readers of this book would subscribe to that 'significant minority' and so begin this chapter at Keighley.

The location of the station was determined by the junction between the main line and the branch. There are two long platforms curving slightly towards Leeds and two shorter ones curving more sharply and on a rising gradient towards Oxenhope. The main buildings front onto the road bridge above. There is direct access by ramp from road level to each platform without the need to negotiate stairs. Half way up the ramp there is a footbridge which does involve steps.

When I first arrived at Keighley by train in 1963, from Frizinghall, there was still a ticket barrier by the exit from the booking hall above platforms 1 and 2 and passengers were channelled that way onto the footbridge. At that time all four platforms retained canopies and there was a tea room on platform 2. The whole place was very shabby not having been painted for ages. Lighting was by small electric lights with tiny yellow tin signs proclaiming 'Keighley'. The station never aspired to the orange totems which adorned some of its neighbours.

For a long time after the Worth Valley reopening, the main line part of the station continued to deteriorate. It was eventually tidied up in 1978, then immediately made to look deliberately shabby to create a wartime atmosphere for the filming of 'Yanks'.

Meanwhile in 1968, Worth Valley trains had begun to run into platform 4, the only one to retain even part of its canopy which was cut back as long ago as 1955. For the first eight years, trains had to propel about ¼ mile out of the station in order for the engine to run round. BR still used platform 3 occasionally. Then at Easter 1976, Worth Valley tracks were extended under the bridge almost to Station Junction Box and the platform 3 line became the run round loop.

No 4 remains the usual departure platform. It is now the only one to retain original features though it is hoped that eventually the rather bare No 3 may be restored to a similar standard with canopies. The original waiting room and toilets are in use on platform 4 as are two rooms under the ramp now housing the Station Master and the relics shop of the Vintage Carriages Trust. The buffet and shop operate from a kiosk installed during 1990. This replaced a similar but narrower structure which had given service for 20 years since being acquired from Ilkley Station.

Platform 4 was extended by two coach lengths in 1970/71, previously it used to end some way short of the water tower.

On Sundays during the summer of 1968 Worth Valley customers gained access to the station through the derelict carriage sidings at the back of platform 4 because BR insisted on keeping the station locked at times when their appalling Sunday service was not running. Happily

Platform 4 retains part of its canopy but No 3 is rather bare. 79964 awaits departure for Oxenhope.   *(John Bateman)*

May Wilkinson dispenses a cup of tea from her new (1990 built) kiosk.   *(Martin Bairstow)*

'Fred', an 0-6-0 saddle tank similar to BR class J94, leaving Keighley during a snowstorm in March 1976.   *(John Sagar)*

that problem was resolved fairly quickly. Rail access to the carriage sidings had been through an arch in the Station Bridge. By 1980 the site was well and truly derelict. Then the West Yorkshire PTE arranged to lease it back from the KWVR, who were in turn leasing it from BR, in order to provide a car park for both BR commuters and Worth Valley customers.

The latest addition to Keighley Station came in 1990 with the recommissioning of a locomotive turntable on the original site near to the end of platform 3. The machine is the celebrated turntable from Garsdale which used to turn pilot engines on the Settle & Carlisle line. It is pictured on the rear cover of *Railways Around Harrogate Volume Two*.

The signal box occupies the site of Keighley West Box. The present cabin used to be at Esholt Junction on the Ilkley line. It has not yet been brought into operation.

Departure from Keighley starts with a 1 in 58 gradient and the line quickly turns through 90 degrees. When the rails are wet heavy trains can easily slip. They no longer have the facility enjoyed by freight trains pre-1962 of setting back beyond the station and taking a run at it. If the loco is struggling it will begin to surmount the problem when it rounds the curve by the Globe Inn.

The YEB depot on the right is the one time Great Northern Railway goods station. The GNR route to Bradford and Halifax used to start here, go under the Worth Valley line by a bridge, now filled in, then run parallel but at a steeper gradient for over two miles past GN Junction, through its own station at Ingrow, eventually disappearing into Lees Moor Tunnel.

At GN Junction there was a single track connection between the two railways allowing passenger trains to travel from Keighley Station on to the GNR route. The layout here was controlled by a signalbox of Midland origin which also issued the single line token to the driver of Worth Valley trains. When the GN route first opened, three signalboxes were required to operate this complex. A Midland box near to the Globe Inn controlled a conventional double track junction signalling Worth Valley trains to a smaller box ¼ mile further on called Single Line Junction and sending Bradford trains to Keighley Goods Junction, the corresponding GN box where the passenger and goods lines converged, both double track.

Approaching Ingrow, there is on the right-hand side the Vintage Carriage Museum soon to be joined by a new locomotive workshop following the re-location of the Bahamas Locomotive Society from Dinting.

For the first twenty years after reopening, Ingrow Station (1¼ miles) was something of an embarrassment. Badly vandalised during closure, the best that the Society could do was to tidy it up and use it as an unstaffed request stop.

One Sunday morning early in 1986, my German lesson on television was interrupted by a 'phone call from David Pearson, now a Vice Chairman of the Society. He was carrying out a Council instruction to consult me in my professional capacity regarding the wording of a proposed appeal for donations from the membership. I approved his wording but questioned whether he really understood that the amount he sought to raise was greater than the sum total of all donations since 1962. David claimed to be aware of this but said that he had to give it a chance.

Ex L&Y 0-6-0 No. 52044, dating from 1887, prepares to leave Keighley on 14 August 1977 in the company of Great Northern 'Atlantic' No. 990 'Henry Oakley', a veteran of 1898 which was used on the Worth Valley for just one year. *(Larry Goddard)*

During 1989, the former Garsdale Turntable was installed on the old turntable site at Keighley. The Railway's 50 ton crane was in charge of the operation on 18 November. *(John Sagar)*

'Jinty' No 47279 being turned on 28 October 1990. *(John Sagar)*

The 'new' Ingrow Station (ex-Foulridge) is superior to its predecessor and more compatible with other Worth Valley Stations. *(Martin Bairstow)*

What he was after was to raise funds to purchase the Midland station building from Foulridge closed in 1959, on the Skipton to Colne line, transport it to Ingrow and rebuild it stone by stone. A short time later it was learned that one individual, Mr Geoffrey Reeday, was willing to underwrite the entire scheme. In fact there were other donations but Mr Reeday provided about 85% of the funds. Apparently he had considered restoring a loco-motive but that had been done before so he decided that a station would be a more permanent memorial.

The result is there to see. Not only has the old Foul-ridge building been incorporated into the refurbished station but, thanks to a joint venture with Bradford Council, the station yard and forecourt has been paved in sets and the entrance adorned with the massive iron gates which used to belong to Keighley Goods Yard. The station is now staffed and all trains stop. The Vintage Carriage Museum and, eventually, the 'Bahamas' complex complete the Ingrow Railway Centre.

The platform at Ingrow leads directly into the 150 yard tunnel. Immediately at the other end of this, on the right, is Clough's Mill which had a private siding up until closure of the branch.

Once clear of the mill complex, the setting becomes rural and remains so more or less for the rest of the journey. Standing just before the bridge over the River Worth near mile post 1½ is the distant signal for Damems. This hasn't been 'pulled off' since 1962 but it still serves as a permanent reminder that drivers must be prepared to stop at the home signal protecting the level crossing nearly half a mile ahead.

Damems (2 miles) is often referred to as 'the smallest full size station in England'. The platform is just one coach length. It opened in 1867 a few months after the railway itself to serve a small mill nearby. There was once a siding on the site now occupied by the Station House. Only a few trains called at Damems which closed in May 1949. In latter BR days, the only structure on the platform was a hut for the protection of the relief cross-ing keeper who attended when the regular incumbent had any time off.

From 1928 until closure, the level crossing was opened, by hand, by Mrs Annie Feather who lived in the station house and operated the signals from a ground frame in her front garden. She continued to occupy the house in her enforced retirement until well into Society days. It is now let to a Society member.

In 1971 the signal frame was transferred to the small cabin acquired from Earby Gates on the then recently closed Skipton to Colne line – ex Midland of course. The present station building arrived in 1983 having pre-viously served as a checker's hut at Keighley Goods Yard.

With a ticket-cum-station masters office, waiting room, toilet, signal box and house still in railway ownership, the claim to be a 'full size' station seems justified. It is doubtful it would be there at all but for the level crossing which carries very little road traffic.

It was the length of straight track beyond Damems which the Society decided, in 1971 offered the best site for a passing loop. This was badly needed to double the carrying capacity of the line. After two years of hand signalling, the ex Midland box from Frizinghall was moved to Damems Junction (2¼miles). The title may appear to overstate the case but it was the practice on the Midland Railway to christen anything a junction where there was so much as a cross over or a loop.

Oakworth (2¾ miles) is the railway's period piece. Being a good half mile from the village which is at the top of a hill, the station is rather a quiet spot off the tourist trail. There have been no commercial pressures to turn waiting rooms into shops or buffets. Instead the station has been restored to something like Edwardian appearance with lantern style gas lamps, enamel signs and various items of platform furniture such as milk churns and a Midland Railway coffin trolley.

The station survived the period of closure very well. At Spring Bank Holiday 1965, I joined a small party of members who travelled on a motorised permanent way trolley from Haworth to Oakworth. The Society was breaking new ground having just acquired the keys to Oakworth Station. Whilst part of the team drove the trolley on some pretext to GN Junction, then as far as it could go, two or three of us entered the booking office, possibly the first human beings to do so in almost three years.

Everything was just as it had been left. There was even a half full bottle of ink. A large round table in the middle of the office had been tipped over, presumably in disgust, and the contents lay in a corner. Amongst this pile of rubbish were old ticket ledgers and correspondence including requests from York to explain why trains had been stopped at signals. Even I knew the answer to that. Instructions were still exhibited on the wall that the level crossing was to be opened on receipt

of telephone advice of an approaching train from GN Junction Box or Haworth Station. Clearly the man had been too slow and had failed to 'pull off' the signal in time. Perhaps he had been asleep. In those days BR could afford to employ headquarters staff to follow up such enquiries.

Prior to 1956, Oakworth had a passing loop with a signal box at the Keighley end of the station. There was no facility to cross two passenger trains. This is why Oakworth was not considered suitable for a passing loop after reopening. The Railway would have needed to purchase additional land in order to widen the formation and build a second platform.

It is sometimes suggested that the permanent way depot in what was Oakworth Goods Yard blends in badly with the restored station but it is kept at least as tidy as any old coal yard would have been.

Leaving Oakworth, the railway passes over a series of well built stone bridges including the three arch Mytholmes Viaduct crossing the River Worth. This is the 1892 deviation built by the Midland Railway. Below on the left is the dried up overgrown bed of the Vale Mill Dam which the railway originally crossed on a timber viaduct. Beyond the short Mytholmes Tunnel, there is a sharp curve by which the deviation rejoins the original alignment. We are now in the valley of the Bridgehouse Beck which flows through Oxenhope to join the River Worth near Mytholmes Viaduct.

Haworth Station (3¾ miles) lies at the foot of the village which is reached by the footbridge beyond the end of the platform. Outwardly at least, the station is in original form but the waiting and ladies' rooms have

'Black Five' 4-6-0 No. 45212, emerging from Ingrow Tunnel in 1977. No. 45212 was purchased direct from BR at Lostock Hall, Preston from where it had worked the last scheduled BR steam train to Blackpool on 4 August 1968. *(Larry Goddard)*

The claim that Damems is the smallest 'full size' station in England rests on it boasting all the usual facilities, booking office, waiting room, toilets and signal box. *(Martin Bairstow)*

Class S160 No 5820 between Damems Junction and Oakworth on 24 September 1988. Built by Lima, Ohio in 1945, No 5820 seems to have gone direct to Poland where it was located by KWVR Members.

(D. Stuart Lindsey)

The other stations may present a 1950s BR image but at Oakworth the style is of the Midland period.
(Martin Bairstow)

Haworth Station in the Autumn of 1977 with standard 4-6-0 No. 75078 about to depart for Keighley. The wooden platform extension built about the turn of the century is evident. *(Larry Goddard)*

The oldest engine on the Worth Valley line, 0-6-0 well tank 'Bellerophon', is seen tackling the last half mile into Oxenhope. Dating from 1874 'Bellerophon' sees occasional passenger service. Its restoration is described in the chapter on the Vintage Carriages Trust. *(John Sagar)*

been turned into a souvenir and bookshop. This is not an ideal arrangement because the shop is not big enough and yet it consumes most of the space otherwise available to protect waiting passengers from the elements.

Next to the door leading outside is a small plaque in memory of the late Edgar Chapman, Station Master from 1965 until 1981. He was a Vice Chairman of the Society from its formation until his death and, for many years after the reopening, was in charge of cashing up for all stations and taking the money to the Bank. So indispensable was Edgar in this regard that he was replaced first by a volunteer rota and eventually by Securicor. Mrs Hylda Chapman ran a sweet shop from part of the booking office which was remodelled for the purpose but has since changed back again.

While Edgar ruled Haworth, the writ of the Stations Committee applied everywhere else but not there. Geoffrey Lewthwaite, now the Railway's most senior booking clerk, was kept out of Haworth booking office for the first ten years after reopening. Edgar and Hylda devoted their retirement almost exclusively to the Worth Valley Railway. In 1979 some visiting BR officials were surprised to learn that Edgar had not yet sampled their then comparatively new High Speed Diesel Train. On further enquiry they were astounded to learn that Edgar had not been to London since the War and Hylda had never been. The omission was soon rectified in fitting style courtesy of BR.

The Society was fortunate to inherit a sizeable yard at Haworth complete with large goods warehouse. This was used to house the first locomotive acquisitions and in due course became the workshop.

For many years members of the Loco Department worked in appalling conditions. To a considerable extent they still do because much remains to be done to provide adequate workshop and volunteer facilities.

The first inspection pit was dug in 1969 to be followed by a second larger one in 1974. The new shed project began in 1979 but was initially frustrated by a dispute with the contractor. After a pause, work resumed and, for the first time, the Society secured outside financial assistance. This came first from the English Tourist Board and then from the West Yorkshire Metropolitan County Council.

Prior to 1970, the area between the station and the goods yard, was occupied by a cornmill with a circular row of shops fronting on to the station. I remember getting a discount in a Corner Café there back in 1965 because I was working to reopen the Railway — the organisation which eventually bought the site and turned it into a car park!

Visible from the train soon after leaving Haworth Station are the two sleeping cars parked at the near end of the shed. These are used as accommodation for working members who live too far away to get home (or, some might say, who spend so much time at the Railway that they get locked out). More seriously, it is a considerable help for members who are working early turns or lighting up engines particularly on consecutive days.

The loop at Haworth extending some way beyond mile post 4 is now used only for access to the yard. Prior to 1956 it was signalled as a passing loop.

At the time of closure, Oxenhope (4¾ miles) had just one coal siding. There was no longer any track into the stone goods shed adjoining the station platform which had already succumbed to vegetation emerging between the flagstones. It was a sleepy branch line terminus.

The station buildings are smaller than at Haworth. A shop has appeared in what was the booking office in BR days. That function has been transferred across the booking hall to the former Station Master's office.

In other respects Oxenhope has changed out of all recognition. In 1970, the 'White Shed' opened. This was a double track 120 foot extension to the goods warehouse adjoining the platform and originally intended as a locomotive running shed. This idea was abandoned in favour of keeping the loco department at Haworth. Instead the 'White Shed' has been used for carriage restoration. It was extended a further 100 feet in 1976.

The three road 'Green Shed' opened in two stages in 1971 and 1973. This provides a home mainly for locomotives which are out of traffic long term but which are in sufficiently good external condition to appear as static exhibits.

Since the late 1970s Oxenhope has been the base for operational coaches. There are two sidings with a carriage washing platform in between.

The headshunt was extended in 1971 to allow two locomotives to run round together. The area beyond the new buffers was then landscaped to make a car park. This and the station approach have been paved in sets thanks to a joint initiative with Bradford Council. A picnic area has been created on the far side of the headshunt.

Prior to 1988, the platform outside the main building was nearly a foot lower than the rest. This defect was put right and the entire platform resurfaced. Badly eroded platform edging stones were replaced by stones recovered from stations at Thongs Bridge, on the Holmfirth branch, and from Ilkley.

The Station House is still in Railway ownership. Since being vacated by the last BR Station Master in 1970, it has been the residence of Jack and Dora Rowell, two stalwart supporters of the Society.

For many years, there was discussion on how best to offer a catering facility at Oxenhope. Finally in 1982 a buffet car was purchased from BR and positioned permanently between the stone shed and the station building with access from the platform. From here customers may obtain take away drinks and snacks or may partake of sit down meals.

How to find the station from the cobbled Main Street in Haworth. This sign has been there a considerable time. In 1991 the Railway sponsored a minibus service, free to rail passengers, between station and village on Sundays and Bank Holidays.
(Martin Bairstow)

79964 accelerates away from Haworth past the sleeping cars which provide overnight accommodation for working members.
(Martin Bairstow)

43924 ready to leave Oxenhope for Keighley in the Spring of 1980. The 'White Shed' is used for carriage restoration. *(Martin Bairstow)*

The Station approach at Oxenhope is now paved in sets, just visible under the snow. The water column was purchased from BR at Skipton and re-erected in 1973. *(Martin Bairstow)*

Signalling

79964 waits for the token to be issued and the starter signal to be lowered, before it can proceed from Damems Junction towards Oxenhope in September 1990.
(Martin Bairstow)

Staffs, tickets and tablets

The most basic system of single line security is the staff. This is a metal object inscribed with the names of the stations or junctions between which it must be carried by the driver of every train. The staff may incorporate the key for the points leading off the main running line into sidings. The locks on the point levers are arranged so that the staff, once inserted, can only be withdrawn when the points are back in their normal position. Thus possession of the staff gives a driver both the authority to be on the single line and the assurance that all points are locked in the correct position.

The staff system is adequate for a short branch line leading to a dead end from which each train will return before another one wishes to enter the branch. It cannot cater, however, for consecutive movements in the same direction.

These are permitted under the staff and ticket system. If a train is expected to be followed by another in the same direction, the signalman shows the staff to the driver but issues him with a ticket. This may be a piece of paper but on many lines it was a metal object of different shape to the staff. An example of a metal ticket is illustrated in *Railways Around Harrogate Volume Two*. The number of tickets available for a particular section of line would be adequate to cater for the likely requirements of traffic that is at least enough to cover the likely number of consecutive trains in one direction. The tickets were strictly controlled, although their function was subordinate to that of the staff.

If a train was to be followed by one in the opposite direction, then the driver would be given the staff and a ticket would not be required. The drawback with the system was the need to predict the direction of the next train movement which might be hours away. If anything unexpected were to arise, the staff might be at the wrong end leading to delays or a long walk for somebody or both.

The ultimate development in nineteenth century single line security was the electric token, sometimes known as a tablet because many of them were round objects. There are token machines in the signal boxes or stations at either end of the section. The number of tokens is unlimited but they are kept inside the machines which are electrically interlocked so that only one token can be withdrawn at a time.

The token may incorporate the key to unlock points at remote locations. To facilitate transfer between signalman and driver, the token is often placed in a pouch attached to a large hoop. In some areas particularly in Scotland there used to be token catchers on the lineside and on the cabs of locomotives to permit transfer at greater speed.

From the 1920s it became the practice to interlock the token machines with the signals so that a train could not be given a clear signal unless a token had been issued.

Eventually in the 1960s it became possible to operate tokenless block whereby the interlocking of the signals alone is relied upon to ensure that there can only be one train in each section at any time. Since then many single lines have been brought within the areas controlled by power boxes and others have been converted to radio signalling. However, both staff and electric token working are still employed on parts of British Railways, on preserved lines and in Ireland. Surprisingly, the principle was never used much in Continental Europe.

Signalling in the Worth Valley

The branch seems to have been worked on the 'one engine in steam' principle with a staff for the first ten years of its existence. Block working was introduced in 1877 with staff and ticket operation from Worth Valley Junction, Keighley to Oxenhope. From 1884 the staff and ticket section was from the Box at Single Line Junction to Oxenhope.

On 4 April 1900, new signal boxes were opened

at Oakworth and Haworth. The line was then worked as follows:

Keighley to Single Line Junction – double track
Single Line Junction to Oakworth – electric token
Oakworth to Haworth – electric token
Haworth to Oxenhope – Staff

A new GN Junction Box replaced Single Line Junction on 24 August 1924.

The passing loops at Oakworth and Haworth were intended to pass two freight trains or one freight and one passenger. There was no second platform at Oakworth. At Haworth the loop was beyond the station towards Oxenhope.

From 1956 until closure the branch was worked as one section from GN Junction to Oxenhope using a staff.

When the line reopened in 1968, the entire branch was operated as one section with a staff. This was kept in the safe in Haworth Station when not in use. With the commissioning of the passing loop at Damems in 1971, temporary arrangements were made to operate each of the two sections with a staff but with the option of keeping the line as one section when the loop was locked out of use.

Permanent signalling came in 1973 when the former Frizinghall signal box opened at Damems Junction and electric token working was introduced.

The staff, now called the 'one train staff' is still used to start each days operation. If only one train is to run, then the staff may be used all day. If it is necessary to open the signal box at Damems Junction, then this is done whilst a train is standing outside the box. The signalman takes the 'one train staff' from the driver and inserts it into his signal frame so as to bring the box into operation. Electric tokens are then issued as required for the sections to Keighley and to Oxenhope.

Normally a driver will pick up a token at Damems Junction and keep it until he has reached the terminus and come back again to the Junction. There the token will be given up to the signalman in exchange for one for the other section. The tokens must be passed through the machines in the signal box. They cannot simply be exchanged between the drivers of passing trains otherwise the starter signals could not be 'pulled off' into the clear position.

There are remote token machines at Oxenhope, Haworth, Oakworth, Ingrow and Keighley. At any of these, a driver who has locked his train into a siding, can report this fact by telephone to the signalman at Damems Junction and then insert his token into the machine. The section is then clear for a fresh token to be issued either at Damems Junction by the signalman or, with his permission, by a driver at one of the remote instruments.

When there remains only one train between Keighley and Oxenhope, Damems Junction box can be closed. The train is stopped outside the box and the driver gives up his token. The signalman shuts down the box, leaving the appropriate signals in the clear position. He withdraws the one train staff from his frame and gives it to the driver who can then continue. When the last locomotive has been locked into the sidings at Haworth, the staff is returned to the safe.

In 1921 the Midland Railway opened a new box at Keighley West to control access into the sidings at Dean Smith & Grace as well as the points at the exit from the station. After withdrawal of the passenger service to Bradford and Halifax in 1955 this box was left switched out most of the time. The Worth Valley trains, being push-pull, did not need the run round facility. After closure in 1962 the box stood derelict until the early 1980s when it was demolished as an eyesore.

Almost immediately, the former box at Esholt Junction on the Ilkley line was purchased and re-erected on the same site as Keighley West. As yet there are no plans to bring it into operation because the Society does not wish to create a post which would need to be manned even for the simplest of train movements. At present the points are crew operated but there is the facility for a ground signalman to take over control on the few occasions that it is necessssary to have shunting movements in Keighley Station without occupying the section to Damems Junction. For this purpose there are a number of ground signals which are normally covered up out of use.

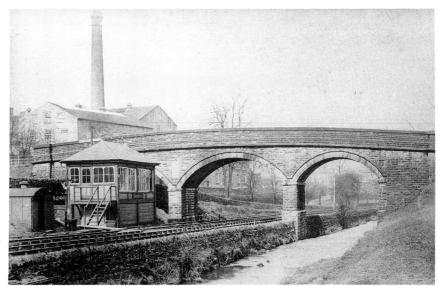

Haworth Signal Box (1900-1956) stood half way along the passing loop some distance from the Station.
(Robin Higgins collection)

The signalman at Keighley G.N. Junction holds up the token for the Oakworth section as the fireman of No 41326 prepares to catch it during the summer of 1955. By the following year the electric token system had given way to a metal staff which was more difficult to transfer without almost stopping.
(Peter Sunderland)

Opened on 24 August 1924, GN Junction Box was distinctly Midland in appearance. It took over the work of three earlier boxes—the old GN Junction, 200 yards nearer to Keighley, Single Line Junction, a short distance nearer to Oxenhope and Keighley Goods Junction on the GNR. The connecting line between the Midland and Great Northern systems was double track from opening on 1 November 1884 until reduced to a single line on 11 October 1942.

The token machine cum block instrument in the Booking Office at Ingrow alongside the omnibus circuit telephone complete with list of ringing codes. *(Martin Bairstow)*

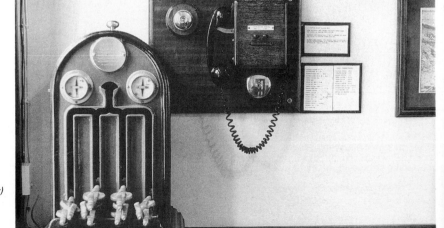

After closure of Oakworth Box in March 1956, the remaining signals were operated from a small ground frame. The repeaters on the panel show the positions of the four ssignals. The wheels behind were used for tightening up the distant signal wires. *(A. M. Ross)*

Ex-GWR 'Prairie' 2-6-2T No 6106 visited the Worth Valley in 1988-89. It is seen running round its train by the new Keighley West box (Ex-Esholt Junction). The shunting signals are worked from a ground frame as the box is not yet commissioned. *(John Bateman)*

47

Train Services from 1968

Over the 20 odd years of Society operation, there has been a trend towards longer trains with more spacious gangwayed coaches and bigger locomotives such as 8F No. 48431, rounding the curve into Oxenhope.

(John Sagar)

The first timetable operating from 30 June 1968 provided for seven trains each way on Saturdays and five on Sundays. From that very first day the pattern was established that a diesel railbus would operate in the morning with a steam train in the afternoon.

After two months it was decided that the service was not ambitious enough. The number of Saturday trains was increased to nine with seven on Sunday. Still that wasn't right. The Saturday service had five diesel trips at hourly intervals. The first one at 8.12 from Oxenhope was too early to attract traffic whilst the fifth one at lunch time could not cope. The next stage was to abandon the first and last trains and to convert the midday one to steam. This seven train service has stood the test of time on Saturdays from March to October and on Sundays in March, April, May and October. Overcrowding on the third diesel trip has prompted a change for 1991 when the diesel will work only the first two journeys and there will be five steam trains.

In the first winter of 1968/69 the normal service continued but there were one or two disasters. For the next winter therefore the Saturday service became all diesel and the Sunday service was restricted to operation between Haworth and Oxenhope. Each turn round at Haworth involved propelling the train part way back to Oxenhope in order to run round, then propelling it back again to the station.

I have to confess that I never understood the reasoning for this 'shuttle' service as it was called. It seemed quite inconsistent with the Railway's oft quoted claim to be a complete branch line. It was not until the late 1980s that a service was resumed over the whole line on Winter Sundays.

In its first six months of operation, the Railway carried 35,000 passengers. This was the number of tickets issued, mostly returns, including members paying half fare but not those using their three annual free tickets. The first full year, 1969, produced over 58,000. In 1970 the figure reached 71,000 but the following year it exceeded 125,000.

The only explanation for this dramatic increase was the release at the end of 1970 of the full length film of *The Railway Children*. Shortly before reopening, the line had featured in a BBC serial based on the classic by E. Nesbit. On that occasion, Oakworth Station had been given a fictitious name. When Lionel Jeffries came to negotiate facilities for his film, the Railway persuaded him to keep the name Oakworth as it was. The effect was dramatic. Money earned for making the film during the Summer of 1970 was minor compared to the passenger revenue generated after its release. Prosperity brought plenty of short term problems. Easter 1971 was chaotic as the Society attempted to cater for the traffic on offer using a seven coach train with a spare engine to speed up the run round at Keighley.

The only solution was to press ahead with the passing loop at Damems in time for the Spring Bank Holiday. Then it became possible to advertise a service of 13 trains per day on Sundays from the end of May to late September and also on Bank Holidays. With minor alterations, this has become the pattern ever since. On these days there is a 40 minute interval throughout the afternoon. The passing loop also enabled the Railway to accommodate special traffic and works trains on days when the advertised service is less intensive.

Midweek operations began during the Summer of 1969 with a service of four trains on Wednesday afternoons in June, July and August. Like the weekend operation this was achieved with an all volunteer staff. During August 1970 the remaining weekdays were filled with the same Haworth to Oxenhope 'shuttle' as on Winter Sundays. This pattern was repeated in 1971.

1972 saw seven day running over the whole branch for the first time albeit for a period of only three weeks in late July/early August. This was followed by two weeks of the previous year's service pattern presumably to compare whether the customers responded better to a full line or a Haworth-Oxenhope only service on Mondays, Tuesdays, Thursdays and Fridays. The issue was resolved and for 1973 there was a full service every day in August. This was extended back to mid July in 1975 and to cover the whole of July and August in 1976.

By this time the number of passengers was exceeding 140,000. It remained at this level, most reluctant to cross the 150,000 barrier until the record year of 1988 when it reached 174,000 since when it has dropped back again slightly.

By 1990 the period of seven day operation had been extended to include the weeks following Easter and Spring Bank Holiday plus ten full weeks from the beginning of July to early September, and also Wednesdays in June. The KWVR shows up BR by operating on Boxing Day then daily until 1 January. Midweek operation is still with all volunteer train crews supplemented by just a handful of employees on stations, shops, catering etc.

The development of weekday services has been a function of the growth in leisure time which affects both the customers and the working members.

In addition to the ordinary timetabled trains, there are a variety of special workings. Through trains from BR probably involve more organisation than they are worth but they do occasionally happen. Of more importance at one time were the train loads of people brought by BR on excursion trains to Keighley. In the 1970s these were marketed as 'Merry Maker' trips in some BR areas. The KWVR used to provide a connecting service. Today such ventures are much rarer as BR have opted out of this business. There are still occasional charter trains.

'Wine & Dine' specials run on a limited number of evenings during the year offering a high standard of catering on the Railway's Pullman train. This comprises a second class Pullman car, an ordinary restaurant car and the Jubilee Bar which was created out of a gutted Mark I carriage. A Sunday lunch service was introduced once a month during the summer of 1990 using additional coaches attached to a timetabled train.

'Santa in Steam' is big business on preserved railways. It began at Haworth on 8 December 1965 when BR granted permission for 'Santa' to travel on board 0-4-0 ST No. 51218 from Haworth Yard to the Station. After the re-opening Santa travelled on timetabled trains on Sundays leading up to Christmas distributing gifts to children. Since 1973 the service has been on trains reserved exclusively for this purpose. The normal service is suspended on Sundays during December.

Another Worth Valley 'first' was the Enthusiast Day held on 17 March 1973. Later extended to cover a full weekend each Spring, the event is based on an intensive timetable using as many different locomotives as possible. In recent years there have also been special weekends in the Autumn. Unfortunately 'Modern Traction' weekends have proved very expensive to stage because of the cost of moving locomotives over BR.

Visiting diesel locomotives outside Haworth new shed in November 1989. Class 14 D9531 and class 24 D5054 are both normally based on the East Lancashire Railway.

(John Sagar)

Connections

Amongst the advantages of the Worth Valley Railway are the excellent connections it enjoys with the main railway network. Some preserved railways are barely accessible by public transport but at Keighley there are now more trains than ever before serving the BR side of the station with the prospect of further improvements to come.

The weekday service to Leeds is half hourly, taking half an hour and giving connections to most parts of the country. There is an hourly service to Bradford, whilst there are three trains an hour to Skipton, Shipley and to stations in between. There are six trains per day through to Carlisle and four to Lancaster. In all cases the Sunday frequency is about half the weekday level.

Passengers originating from Liverpool, Manchester, Blackpool and Preston directions may travel by train to Hebden Bridge whence there is a bus from outside the station to Oxenhope. This operates up to four times a day on Saturdays throughout the year and every day in summer, taking passengers over the 1,400 feet summit of Cock Hill.

On summer Sundays and Bank Holiday Mondays there is a bus from Burnley, Nelson and Colne direct to Haworth Station. There is an hourly service daily from those East Lancashire towns to Keighley.

Within the West Yorkshire PTE area, train and bus fares are well below the national average, especially outside the Monday to Friday peak periods. 'Metro Cards' issued for periods of between one week and one year are available on all BR trains and most buses within the County (and give a discount on the KWVR). There is also a Day Rover Ticket costing only £1.40 in 1990. Saver Strips giving 12 journeys for the price of 10 can be used on either bus or train.

For customers arriving at the Worth Valley by car there is free parking at Keighley, Ingrow and Oxenhope stations. There is a charge at Haworth where parking is at a premium, otherwise the station yard would be full of non railway customers.

As far as possible, the KWVR would like to be in the business of bringing tourists into Haworth by train thereby relieving traffic congestion rather than have them arrive by car and go for a train trip later. Hence the encouragement to park at other stations.

Since 1987, most services on the 'main line' through Keighley have been in the care of 'pacer' diesel multiple units. A class 144 waits to leave for Bradford.
(Martin Bairstow)

Fares

A complaint sometimes levied at preserved railways is that their fares are too high for 'ordinary' passengers, that so they function only as a tourist amenity but cannot possibly be taken seriously as a form of transport. There is an undoubted truth in this charge as regards many preserved lines but the KWVR has taken a number of steps to counter it.

Certainly, an ordinary return from Keighley to Oxenhope costs more than would a journey of comparable length on BR. However, senior citizens have enjoyed half price since long before BR invented a railcard. Children travel free under five and at half fare under 16 and there is a family fare. Prams and bicycles are carried free of charge.

There is a small discount for holders of PTE Metro cards and day rovers or any BR rover ticket whose validity includes Keighley. Members of the Preserva-

tion Society can obtain three free day tickets per annum. Any additional trips cost half fare.

Tourist passengers get more for their money than just a train journey. They enjoy all the trappings of a preserved railway—the restored locomotives, carriages and stations, not to mention the museum at Oxenhope which is free to rail ticket holders.

These additional facilities are of little value to local residents who may for example wish to use the trains for shopping. For many years the Railway's answer was to encourage them to join the Society but this did not seem to work. So in 1986 a local residents railcard was introduced. It is issued free to residents of Keighley and the villages in the Worth Valley and entitles the holder to travel at half the ordinary fare (or one quarter if the holder is also a member of the Society, but **not** an eighth if he/she is also a child or senior citizen!)

The card has proved quite successful not only in helping to fill trains but in forging a better relationship between the Railway and the local community.

A facility whose take up rate has been more disappointing is the ability to book through to Oxenhope from any station on BR. In relation to the number of people actually changing trains at Keighley, the issue of through tickets has been negligible. One explanation may be that many travellers hold either a Metro Card or some kind of BR Rover Ticket or are members of the Preservation Society. The other reasons is that neither the public nor BR staff expect the facility to be available so they assume that it isn't.

In the past most through booking facilities have been short lived. They have died for want of sufficient use to justify the cost of manual administration. Now that BR has its APTIS system, there is no reason why tickets should not as a matter of course be sold to destinations on preserved railways or to places reached by bus or ship. Only when this becomes a generally accepted principle will people take it seriously. 'One off' facilities can be more trouble than they are worth. BR would probably complain that some preserved railways and more especially deregulated bus operators will not discipline themselves to abide by terms agreed for any worthwhile length of time—another charge which the KWVR would deny.

 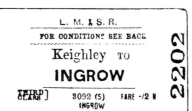 

The KWVR does now issue card tickets but they are accounted for via a cash register unlike these older examples which used to be accounted for manually.

(Geoffrey Lewthwaite collection)

Ex LMS class 8F No. 8431 leaving Haworth for Oxenhope on 6 August 1977. Built at Swindon in 1944, this locomotive languished in Barry scrapyard from 1964 until 1972. The Worth Valley had it running again by 1975.

(Larry Goddard)

51

Whatever happened to the Commuter service?

That this question is so seldom asked may in itself largely provide the answer. There doesn't seem to have been much demand expressed for it.

When closure of the Worth Valley branch was being canvassed from 1959, the official story was that it had outlived its usefulness but that other routes including the 'Main Line' through Keighley had a secure future and were to be modernised. Clearly the founder members of the Preservation Society rejected this view. Their declared aim was to restore to the Worth Valley the type of passenger and goods service still being provided on the adjacent railways.

As far as freight is concerned, the idea now seems ridiculous. Since 1981 there hasn't even been a goods facility at Keighley at which traffic could be exchanged. The days of the branch pick up goods are long vanished.

Railway commuters, on the other hand, are very much alive and well. Phenomenal growth in car ownership, far from eliminating the need for railways, has proved the very reason why more and better railway facilities are needed in conurbations throughout Europe —including West Yorkshire.

This was rather less apparent in 1968. The six years during which the Worth Valley was closed had seen a terrible contraction in the British Railways network in which almost all similar branch lines had gone. At Keighley it looked as though the service to Bradford might soon disappear and there was no guarantee that the Leeds to Skipton line had any long term future. This was hardly the moment to relaunch a commuter service to the relatively tiny village of Oxenhope. Understandably the Preservation Society concentrated all its efforts on the tourist potential.

In more recent times numerous local stations have reopened and the West Yorkshire PTE is actively pursuing the reintroduction of passenger services over two freight only lines within its jurisdiction. There is even talk of rebuilding part of the abandoned route from Cross Gates towards Wetherby.

If the day should ever come when PTE plans embrace a commuter service to Haworth and Oxenhope, they would not need to consider the cost of rebuilding, but merely to negotiate a deal with the Keighley & Worth Valley Railway, presumably similar to the Section 20 agreement with BR.

Such speculation is a long way off. Distances within the Worth Valley are very short and road traffic in Keighley is not particularly bad. There must be many residents of Haworth who work in Bradford and Leeds. Almost all own cars. They will drive direct to Bradford, but for Leeds they may well be tempted to park their vehicles at Keighley Station whence there is a good train service which will avoid the traffic problems at Bingley, Shipley, Kirkstall etc, not to mention parking in Leeds. If these customers had the option of a connecting train to Keighley it might not help them much. It could prove slower and less flexible than the option of driving to Keighley Station. It is between Shipley and Leeds where the train really beats the jams, covering in 12 minutes, 11 miles which are difficult by road.

It is more probable that any increase in the scope of train services on the Keighley & Worth Valley Railway will revolve round a progressive extension of the tourist service. It was suggested in a recent discussion document that there are now sufficient tourists around to justify a diesel railbus on those weekdays from March to October which are not yet operated. There was doubt as to whether there were yet sufficient volunteer crews to handle this, but it may come. After all, nobody could have envisaged 25 years ago having sufficient volunteers to cover the level of weekday operation which has been achieved.

The driver and guard exchange farewells with Mr. Jim Sargent, the branch station master, during the last week of passenger service at Oxenhope. There is not a customer in sight for this 'off peak' train.
(Martin Bairstow collection)

Opposite Cloth capped commuters board a Keighley train at Haworth on the first morning of the full diesel service in June 1960. Could a new generation of longer distance commuters help justify a year round Monday to Friday service on the branch?

(Keighley News)

53

Locomotives and Rolling Stock

The first locomotive to arrive at Haworth in January 1965 was the diminutive 0-4-0 saddle tank No. 51218. Built for the Lancashire & Yorkshire Railway in 1901, as a dock shunter. At this very early stage of the Society, the method of watering was a hose pipe.
(Martin Bairstow collection)

It would be way outside the scope of this book to describe all the motive power and carriages on the Keighley & Worth Valley Railway. It could also be unnecessary because the Society itself publishes a Stock Book, a new edition of which compiled by Peter Eastham is due to appear in 1991. The following is but a brief part of the story.

The first engine to arrive at Haworth in January 1965 was the ex Lancashire & Yorkshire Railway 'Pug' No 51218, an 0-4-0 saddletank which had shunted on Liverpool Docks. It was then seriously believed that this engine might haul one or two coaches in passenger service and to that end it was fitted with vacuum brakes.

On 6 March 1965, the Society received its first delivery of rolling stock by rail. No 1247, a Great Northern 0-6-0 saddle tank became the first loco to work over the branch for nearly three years. Its private owner demanded facilities for it which the Worth Valley could not offer and it departed before the reopening. It has appeared on a number of other railways since.

One of the other items brought by No 1247 was the ex L&Y 0-6-0 No 957 (BR No 52044) which had been bought by Tony Cox, then the Secretary but now a Vice President of the Society. This loco, built in 1887, has seen service from time to time but now requires major expenditure if it is to go back into traffic.

A second stock movement at the end of July 1965 brought three Metropolitan coaches which had been made redundant when London Transport electrified to Amersham and Chesham. They had then been purchased privately for possible use on the Westerham branch, a preservation scheme which failed to get off the ground. The three coaches were destined to provide the mainstay of Worth Valley passenger stock for the first few years after reopening. Eventually they were given to the Vintage Carriages Trust for authentic restoration.

It had always been the Society's intention to operate diesel as well as steam trains. On 19 March 1966, the experimental 500hp diesel electric No D0226 arrived on permanent loan from English Electric. During that

Saturday afternoon, it worked a passenger service for members only between Haworth and Oxenhope alternately with a steam locomotive, N2 No 4744, affording some of us the first chance to ride on the line on a proper train. After that there were fairly regular works trains.

In the early years of the Society, there had been interest in the possibility of acquiring an ex Great Western railcar, then coming up for withdrawal on BR. By the time the Railway could afford such a purchase, the Great Western vehicles were no longer available but more modern BR ones were up for sale. In 1967 two German built Schienenbüsse Nos 79962 and 79964 were purchased for use on off peak services. Two went to the North Norfolk Railway making this BR class of five very well represented in preservation.

For the reopening in June 1968 there were two steam locomotives of adequate size available for traffic. Both had been purchased privately as the Railway had no funds. Ivatt 2-6-2T No 41241 represented a type which had regularly worked the branch in the 1950s. It was bought by the late W Hubert Foster and Ron Ainsworth, who subsequently sold it to the Society. 'USA' 0-6-0T No 30072 was and still is owned by Richard Greenwood, the KWVR Company Chairman.

Towards the end of 1968, with these two engines out of traffic for repairs, the Society was obliged to press into service the 2-6-0 'Crab' No 42700 which was on permanent loan from the National Collection but hardly fit for proper use. It took almost two hours to get from Keighley to Oxenhope on one miserable Saturday in December 1968.

The National Collection comprised locomotives preserved by BR and its predecessors and now belongs to the Museum in York. 42700 remained on the Worth Valley as a static exhibit until 1977 when it was exchanged for the Great Northern 'Atlantic' 4-4-0 No 990 'Henry Oakley'. This was in working order but stayed for only one year during which the Worth Valley made occasional use of this prestigious East Coast Main Line loco dating from 1898.

Another visitor from the National Collection was 9F 2-10-0 No 92220 'Evening Star'. This was the last steam locomotive built for British Railways in 1960. Withdrawn as early as 1965, it worked on the Worth Valley branch for two years from 1973 before 'retiring' again to York Museum.

The reopening of the Worth Valley branch came only six weeks before the end of steam operation on BR. Many classes had already disappeared. Shortly before his death in 1977, Hubert Foster told me that he had been ready to purchase at least one more suitable branch line engine. If the light railway order had come in 1967, he would have done so, but by 1968 they had all gone.

The Society invested its first years profit in 'Black Five', No 45212, which had been one of the last locos to run on BR. It was also able to secure 'Standard' 2-6-4T No 80002 which had enjoyed a short lease of life as a stationary steam heating boiler thereby bridging the gap between the BR steam and preservation eras. That, most people thought, was it as far as ex BR locos were concerned.

There were still plenty of steam locomotives in industrial use. The Society bought 'Fred', a 0-6-0 saddle-tank similar to BR class J94 from the Coal Board. Various members bought no fewer than three 54 ton 0-6-0 saddletanks from Stewarts & Lloyds at Corby. Such engines were functional particularly with the low speeds required on the Worth Valley branch. They were not as aesthetically pleasing as main line locomotives.

There was in South Wales a scrap merchant called Dai Woodham who received hundreds of withdrawn steam locomotives into his yard at Barry. In 1967, it was noticed that whilst all the ex Midland 0-6-0 freight engines had been withdrawn, there was an example, No 43924, still at Barry in apparently reasonable condition. Eight individuals formed themselves into the Midland 4F Society, bought the loco and had it delivered to the Worth Valley where it entered traffic in 1970.

No 43924, which was eventually transferred to KWVR ownership in 1990, became the first of approximately 200 locomotives to emerge from Barry scrap-

Midland 1F 0-6-0T No. 1708 was representative of a type which had worked the branch in earlier days. Unfortunately it operated only one passenger turn for the Society before moving on.
(Peter Hutchinson)

Midland 0-6-0 tank engines were the staple motive power on the branch from about 1875. In 1883 five locomotives of this type, numbered 218, 219, 1397, 1398 and 1399, were allocated to Keighley. They were quite advanced for the period having overall cabs to protect the crews from the Worth Valley weather. During the 1930s, the 0-6-0s gave way to Midland 0-4-4 tanks which were push-pull fitted. These were the mainstay of the Worth Valley passenger service until the arrival of the Ivatt 2-6-2 tanks.

Great Northern J52 0-6-0 saddle tank No. 1247 was the first engine to arrive on the Worth Valley in steam in 1975. Agreement could not be reached with its owner so it never worked a passenger train.
(Martin Bairstow collection)

yard over the next 20 years. It was also the first to be restored to traffic. As time went on each successive engine rescued was in a worse and worse state. There are still many of them up and down the country requiring restoration. The KWVR has restored six ex-Barry locos. The only snag in the Barry saga is that the large number of steam locomotives preserved nationally is so heavily representative of the classes which went to Barry. Types which were sent to other scrapyards tended to get broken up.

There was yet another source of steam locomotives. Although most Continental trains are too large to fit under our bridges there is obviously no problem with locomotives built to run in this country provided, of course, that you remove any additional attachments such as extra large cabs for operation within the Arctic Circle.

In 1973 a group led by Richard Greenwood purchased 2-8-0 No 1931. This had started life very much like one of the BR 'WD' class but it was sent to the Netherlands at the end of the Second World War and they in turn sold it to Sweden. It now belongs to the Society and it is hoped one day to restore it as an authentic BR 'WD' – a class which had otherwise escaped preservation.

A year or two later, Richard Greenwood was amongst a party of Worth Valley members who went to Poland and purchased for the Society an S 160 2-8-0. Built in America from 1942, some of the class ran in England for two years before going to Europe after D Day. No 5820 now sees regular use in the Worth Valley.

The provision of coaching stock has been slightly less adventurous. In 1969 the Society acquired a set of four suburban coaches from Kings Cross. Since then the trend has been to standardise on BR suburban and Mark I stock for ordinary services. At first such vehicles were regarded as dispensable but when they became no longer available from BR the policy changed to one of maintaining them for posterity.

Normal passenger services are operated either by steam train or, at quiet times, by one of the two Waggon & Machinenbau diesel railbuses. Diesel loco hauled trains have never featured in the regular timetable but, especially since acquisition of the Class 25 D5209, it has been possible to cover emergencies, including occasions when traffic is too much for a 56 seat diesel railbus.

A number of the steam locomotives remain privately owned either by individuals or by groups. The Society learnt at an early stage, possibly over No 1247, of the ever present risk that a loco may be taken elsewhere. Each locomotive is therefore subject to a medium to long term agreement that the KWVR will repair it and the owners will keep it where it is. In the case of 'City of Wells' the agreement provides for the KWVR to maintain it to branch line standards but for the owners to stand the extra cost of making it suitable for running on BR. Quite naturally absences for BR running are provided for in the Worth Valley agreement. Appropriate arrangements have also been made to protect the interests of both the KWVR and the Bahamas Locomotive Society following the arrival in 1990 of the 'Jubilee' class 'Bahamas' and the ex LNWR Coal Tank No 1054 from their previous home at Dinting.

LMS 'Crab' 2-6-0 No. 2700 was on loan from the National Railway Museum from 1968 until 1977, however, it saw little service.
(Peter Hutchinson)

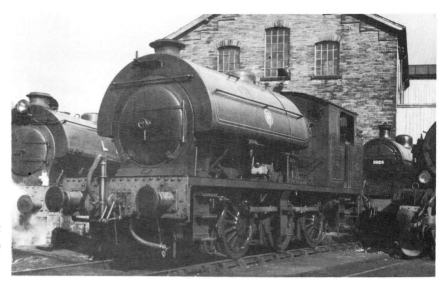

62 was one of three identical 0-6-0 saddle tanks purchased by Worth Valley members from Stewarts & Lloyds at Corby in 1969. No. 62 was sold in 1982 but 57 'Samson' and 63 'Corby' are retained.   *(Peter Hutchinson)*

J72 0-6-0T No. 69023 'Joem' was built in 1951 to an 1898 design. Since leaving the Worth Valley in 1975, it has turned up on a number of preserved railways.
(Peter Hutchinson)

Having missed an opportunity to purchase a 'Jinty' direct from BR for lack of funds pre-1968, the South Yorkshire 3F Society eventually restored No 47279. Built in 1924, this locomotive spent 12 years in Barry Scrapyard from where this group purchased it in 1979, minus many vital parts, including a chimney. It re-entered traffic in 1988 and is seen in Oakworth Yard.
(John Sagar)

Midland 4F No. 43924 arriving at Haworth in March 1988. The leading vehicle is an LMS bogie parcels van normally used as a riding van for the permanent way gang and their equipment. *(John Sagar)*

4Fs were no strangers to the branch in earlier days. 44584 approaching Haworth with an Oxenhope to Morecambe excursion on Whit. Monday 1958. *(Peter Sunderland)*

The Organisation

The line was purchased from BR and reopened by the Keighley & Worth Valley Light Railway Ltd. This body is owned as to 90% of its share capital by the Preservation Society. Consequently the Society retains absolute control. This arrangement differs from that of many other preserved railways mainly because the Worth Valley has never had to raise any substantial amount of share capital. For that it has to thank the BR loan agreement which enabled it to buy the line and also the 99% volunteer staffing which allowed income to be ploughed back into the development of the railway once operation was underway.

Control of the Society is vested in a Council of 24 members. The Chairman, Secretary and Treasurer are elected at each Annual General Meeting although, in practice, there has only once been a contest for one of these positions. That was in 1979 when there were two candidates willing to fill the vacancy for Chairman. The three Vice Chairmen and 18 'ordinary' Council members are elected for three year periods, one third of them retiring at each AGM and for these positions it is sometimes necessary to take a ballot.

The Council meets monthly and has done so almost from the beginning of the Society. The December 1990 meeting was the 320th. In the early days the main business was progress (or lack of it) in negotiations for reopening. After that milestone was achieved, Council meetings have been taken up by reports from the various officers and sub-committees and from the directors of the Railway Company.

Many of the sub-committees meet bi-monthly allowing the Council agenda to be kept to manageable lengths. The Chairman and Secretary of each sub-committee are nominated by the Council but any other member may attend and participate in the work of the committee which basically runs a particular department such as Locomotive, Carriage & Wagon, Stations, Catering etc. Any member of the Society may attend Council but only the elected members may vote.

The day to day running of the Railway is supervised by the Management Committee which meets monthly and reports to each Council.

Control over finance is split between the Company Secretary and the Society Treasurer. Basically, the Company receives the train fares and income from catering using these to discharge most operating expenses. Shop takings, car park fees and members' subscriptions are paid into the Society account and used to cover such diverse expenses as wages, staff uniforms and refuse removal. The division of responsibility is largely historical and sometimes arbitrary. The Company pays for electricity and the Society for gas, thus helping to divide the work load fairly evenly.

The person in charge of each days operations is the Responsible Officer. He issues the 'one train staff' to the first train or instructs the driver to obtain it himself from the safe at Haworth. He then remains on the Railway all day directing operations. Normally this is a very dull job unless something goes wrong requiring his presence. If trains run into the evening, a different Responsible Officer is appointed.

The rostering of train crews, signalmen and respon-

LMS 'Black Five' No 5025, seen leaving Oakworth for Oxenhope on 16 July 1972, was based on the Worth Valley for five years pending transfer to the Strathspey Railway in 1974.

(Peter Hutchinson)

sible officers is done three months at a time. Members on the operating list are sent an availability sheet by the rostering officer who then attempts to fill all the positions required. Members aspiring to operating positions are normally expected to have served previously in some less prestigious post. They are given proper training and, in due course, examined to the equivalent of BR standards. On the steam locomotive side, the line of promotion is the traditional cleaner to fireman to driver. In 1968 most of the drivers were ex BR and the Society trained firemen won fairly quick promotion in as little as two years. Now it can take ten years or more for a fireman to become a driver as he must wait for someone to retire or possibly move away from the area in order to create a vacancy.

Stations, sales and buffet staff have their own rostering officer who operates on similar principles. Staff in these departments are given training and are examined on the rules before they can undertake duties such as level crossing keeper which bring them into contact with the trains.

To supplement the volunteer staff, there are a handful of paid positions. All year round there is one full time administrative assistant plus two or three part time staff. The Haworth car park attendant is a paid position on operating days. During the summer, there are about half a dozen temporary posts mainly in sales and buffet. These jobs are filled mainly by students except Keighley buffet, where for many years the Monday to Friday job has been taken by the regular weekend volunteer, Mrs May Wilkinson. The summer temps, other than May, are usually required to earn their keep in addition by walking a mile of track twice a week armed with a big hammer to restore any keys which have fallen out—the traditional platelayer's job.

It will be apparent from the above that nobody is going to jump straight into the driving seat on first becoming a working member. On the other hand, there is every opportunity for new recruits to become involved in whichever aspect of the Railway that suits their interests. There must always be a danger of such an organisation becoming cliquish, forever moaning that it is short of volunteers yet finding nothing to do for new members who do answer the call.

I can only say that in my experience this was not so. When I volunteered my services on a regular basis in the autumn of 1974 a number of members went out of their way to ensure that I was introduced to the workings and politics of the Society. I was given a job in the Sales department and quickly trained as a guard.

Pulling away from Haworth on 22 October 1977, standard class 4MT No. 75078. Built as late as 1956, this loco lasted only ten years in BR service. It spent six years at Barry scrapyard but was restored to traffic in 1977.

(Larry Goddard)

The Working Members

It must follow that without this gallant band, there would be no Keighley & Worth Valley Railway. Other people play important parts – the general membership, the customers, the small paid staff and outside contractors but the Railway is maintained, managed and operated almost 99% by those members who volunteer their time and skills.

There is (or was) in my office some old correspondence from the Inland Revenue who argued that those who volunteered to work on a preserved railway did so not out of any charitable motive but out of pure self interest. The issues at stake were something into which I will not digress except to compliment one of Her Majesty's Inspectors of Taxes on summing up so accurately why people volunteer to work on the Railway – because they want to.

Despite their apparent selfish motivation, the working members of this and other railways have given enormous pleasure to many people and in the process have made a significant contribution to their local economies.

But who are the individuals who make up the volunteer workforce and what possesses them to get involved in this particular activity?

I have chosen six individuals representing different age groups, all of course with an interest in railways but in different branches of the subject. If there is a slight bias in the selection, it is towards members who have assisted with some of my earlier publications.

Robin Higgins

Inevitably, there are only a handful of members who have been actively involved throughout the Society's 29 years to date. One of this select group is Robin Higgins, a native of Barnoldswick where he still lives and works.

Now in Lancashire, Barnoldswick used to be in the West Riding of Yorkshire which may explain why Robin attended Keighley Grammar School. Each afternoon he returned home by the Bradford to Carlisle 'slow' leaving Keighley at 4.02 and changing onto the 4.30 Barnoldswick at Skipton. Across the platform at Keighley, the 4.05 Worth Valley departure would be waiting, formed of a push-pull set powered by an Ivatt 2-6-2T just like on the Barnoldswick branch.

Robin took the first opportunity of a half day holiday to travel to Oxenhope and back. He repeated the trip on a number of occasions until, finally, or so he thought, he joined the last dmu at 11.15 pm on the snowy evening of Saturday 30 December 1961. At that stage he didn't know that preservation was being seriously canvassed.

Robin was and still is a member of the Ffestiniog Railway. His first holiday away from parents was a fortnight in Wales spend one week travelling the BR lines with a rover ticket and one week working on the Ffestiniog. But for practical and financial reasons, the Ffestiniog was out of reach as a more regular pursuit. When he learnt of the meeting at the Temperance Hall, called to launch the Worth Valley, the attraction was obvious. Robin was in attendance but he was a bit slow at paying a subscription, thus missing out on a now coveted membership number below 100.

That false economy apart, Robin has been active in the Society throughout, serving on the Council for most of the time. Early in 1965, the embryonic retail sales

Robin has a brush with the law during a campaign to promote rail safety for children in November 1989. *(John Sagar)*

department was in need of some kind of co-ordination, so Robin was appointed Sales Manager. He has retained an interest in this side of things ever since, chiefly through his publishing of colour postcards. He has been responsible for most of the Society's extensive collection of well over 200 cards.

Before turning to colour, Robin was trying to earn a few coppers for the Society by selling black & white postcards on a BR rail tour. He encountered a potential customer in the form of Richard Greenwood who enquired whether the Worth Valley branch was in fact going to reopen. Richard had launched the L & Y Saddletanks Fund which would soon be looking for a home for its purchase – the diminutive 'Pug' No 51218. Robin extended an invitation which produced for the Worth Valley both its first locomotive and its solicitor, though he suspects that they might have turned up anyway.

Robin drove the first diesel railbus in passenger service on Sunday 30 June 1968, the day after the reopening. Later he took a sideways promotion onto the steam footplate passing as a fireman during the summer of 1969 and a driver 5½ years later.

In 1974, he was amongst a group of members who visited Poland where they located and eventually purchased and brought back home the Austerity S160 class 2-8-0. This exploit is described in Robin's book *Over Here*. He has contributed to a number of Worth Valley publications and was for nearly ten years during the 1980s the editor of the Society's house magazine *Push and Pull*. He 'retired' from that post at the end of 1989 after producing the one hundredth edition.

Under Robin's editorship, the development of the magazine was continued. It was he who introduced colour photography on a regular basis. Together with his two predecessors, Bob Cryer and Mike Goodall, Robin succeeded in getting the magazine out every quarter for 25 years. There has never been a need to publish an apology for non-appearance or late delivery. Robin's wife Marjorie is also active on the railway, mainly in the catering department.

John Bradley

Following its inaugural meeting on 1 March 1962 the Society sent details of its aims to the railway press in the hope of recruiting additional members. In terms of numbers, the response was far from overwhelming but amongst these early recruits were one or two individuals destined to make a significant contribution towards achieving the Society's objectives.

John Bradley joined in the Summer of 1962 in response to a notice in *The Railway Magazine.* Railways were only one of a number of activities enjoyed John who then lived at Bramhope near Leeds. He had travelled on the branch only once in anticipation of its closure. He regretted the disappearance of this and similar lines but had observed with interest the early achievements of preservation in Wales and on the Bluebell Railway. The idea appealed of participating in such a venture nearer to home.

Shortly after joining the Society, John visited Keighley GN Junction where he found the signal box still manned. He exchanged greetings with the incumbent who commented on the irony of this, the largest of Keighley's five boxes, having become the least used. The man was only there waiting for the pick up goods to return from Ingrow East. Soon afterwards the box was closed and the 'branch' to Ingrow East controlled by a staff from Keighley Station Junction.

John had always been interested in signalling. Could he have known then that his newly acquired membership card would eventually put him in charge of a similar job just a little way up the branch? He has been a regular signalman at Damems Junction since it opened in 1973. John has also served as a guard and as a diesel railbus driver since the railway resumed operation in 1968.

Before anybody could indulge in these prestigious duties, someone had to help look after the negotiations

John manages the occasional guard's turn amongst his countless other duties.
(Martin Bairstow)

with BR and the resultant administration which the Railway has created. John was 'roped in' at an early stage to be Membership Secretary of the Society, a post he held for five years. He was involved in forming the operating company and became its first Chairman but quickly transferred to the position of Company Secretary which he has held throughout the operating period. The duties are largely financial but include such tasks as corresponding with the Department of Transport, filing returns etc. For many years he was the Railway's procurer of coaching stock from BR. In consequence John has, in his own words, 'tender' thoughts on this matter.

Hardly a day can pass when John is not involved in one Worth Valley activity or another whether operating trains on the Railway or administering the company at home in the upstairs office from which he has handled the accounts for over 22 years.

He protects the Railway's money as though it were his own. He has never been so annoyed as when BR Estates Department charged £80 for serving a notice of dilapidations concerning the Worth Valley side of Keighley Station which John considered a joy to behold compared with the eyesore which was the BR station at that time.

Geoffrey Lewthwaite

At the 1981 AGM, when the President called for 'any other business' Geoffrey Lewthwaite rose to his feet to express the opinion that it was lamentable that the Society had not yet appointed an archivist. He confessed to knowing what happens to people who make suggestions. His fears (or aspirations) were fully realised when the Society decided that as a retired librarian he was definitely the right person for the job.

Now he reports to each AGM on his success or otherwise in securing c/o the Bradford City Archivist a complete set of documents relating to the Society's operations, together with whatever material from an earlier age he is occasionally able to pick up.

Geoffrey's interest in railways, dating from his early childhood in the 1920s was inherited from his Father who had been a commuter from Shipley to Armley Canal Road during the years 1904 to 1917.

Geoffrey began taking the *Railway Magazine* in November 1930 but he actually has a complete set of that journal from 1914.

Amongst his early railway travels was a holiday to Jersey in 1931. The family stayed near First Tower Station and made a trip to Corbière and back on the railcar recently transferred from the Jersey Eastern Railway, closed two years previously.

Geoffrey's predominant interest is in railway tickets. In the 1950s Edmondson card tickets were printed by the million each day, but they were collected in at the end of journeys, to the frustration of connoisseurs. He began to assemble his collection systematically in January 1955 at Park Drain, the second station out of Doncaster on the Gainsborough line which closed soon after. Working in the library most Saturdays, opportunities for getting out and about were restricted. On occasions he set off on Friday evening or sometimes by the 3.32 am from Leeds Central to Halifax in order to maximise time in the 'target area' where he travelled from station to station purchasing the odd ticket and taking a photograph – usually just one of each station.

I can vaguely remember an occasion, which I now know to have been on 12 September 1964, when a person came to the booking office at Apperley Bridge enquiring whether there were any LMS tickets still in stock. The answer was no so he contented himself with BR half singles to Manningham and to Shipley. The railman commented to me that he shouldn't have sold him child tickets but he had promised not to use them. Evidently, Geoffrey then took his station photograph upon which I appear from the waist upwards.

Geoffrey waiting for custom at Oakworth where he has booked tickets since 1968.

(J. Shipley)

It was a logical enough step for Geoffrey to join the Worth Valley Society. This happened in 1965 as things were beginning to liven up. Asked why he joined, he replies predictably 'to sell card tickets'. He had to wait rather a long time for that to happen. Initially the Railway relied entirely on bus type tickets issued from a setright machine. That didn't stop Geoffrey from volunteering as a booking clerk. He was rostered for Oakworth on Sunday 30 June 1968, the first day of normal service after the celebrations the previous afternoon. At that time training was less comprehensive than today but Geoffrey was advised to turn up on the

Saturday to familiarise himself with the station and the setright machine.

He's been booking tickets ever since, working up to six or seven days per week during the summer. He somehow finds time also for his music and still travels extensively by train on journeys not just throughout Europe but worldwide.

Geoffrey has submitted both tickets and photographs for inclusion in most of my books. He has also been helpful in sharing his librarian talents by pointing me in the right direction for published material on the most obscure subjects.

John Wright

In May 1983, I joined about 15 Worth Valley members on a trip to Ireland. Discovering that there was a maximum day return fare on Saturdays for any journey, the party decided on taking the longest possible trip – from Dublin to Tralee and back.

Our train comprised a General Motors diesel, followed by that Irish institution, the generator van. Then came three respectable open coaches, a buffet car and to bring up the rear, a rather decrepit corridor brake. The Worth Valley team made a bee line for this last coach. As one member sank into his seat and began to enjoy the third class luxury, he was heard to exclaim: 'I like travelling by train – I could do it all the time.' The retort from John Wright was: 'So do I and I do!'

John is one of a significant minority of working members who also work full time on British Railways. He has been interested in railways since childhood and he considered a railway career when he left school. But in 1968 in the immediate aftermath of the Beeching Period, vacancies were very hard to find at least in this part of the Country.

He joined the Worth Valley just after the reopening in 1968 but didn't take an active part until the end of 1969. After serving his 'apprenticeship' for three years, he was appointed Station Master at Keighley in 1972 – a post he still holds. Involvement with the Worth Valley persuaded John to seek a full time railway job. In 1972 he was offered a vacancy as a parcels porter at Bradford Forster Square, a job which would have ceased to exist in 1981. After a year he moved to Huddersfield as a guard, and he is still there.

Huddersfield crews work local passenger trains to Leeds, Manchester, Wakefield and Sheffield via Penistone. John also went to Clayton West up to the final day in January 1983 when he organised the traditional explosion of fog signals to ensure that the branch did not pass silently into history.

Like many of us, only perhaps more so, John was concerned that the Penistone line itself should not follow the fate of the Clayton West branch. He still finds sufficient of a branch line atmosphere on the Penistone line, although his job is no sinecure. On some trips he is on his feet the whole time issuing tickets. The recent opening of Meadowhall has further increased his business.

John has never aspired to any operating position on the Worth Valley because he wants to do something different to his BR job. His responsibility at Keighley is for the maintenance, cleanliness and general upkeep of the station. He has plenty of support in this but he certainly takes his own share of the dirty work.

63

When on duty, which he shares with other station foremen, John is responsible for the running of the station and for getting the trains away on time. He keeps an eye on BR arrivals and tries to ensure that the Worth Valley departure does not leave if a late running train, which should have connected, is actually approaching Keighley. This task will become a lot harder when the Aire Valley is power signalled as he will no longer be able to tell whether the Keighley signalman has 'pulled off'.

John arrives back at Huddersfield in charge of a dmu from Sheffield via Penistone in November 1984.
(Martin Bairstow)

John says that he has tried to ensure that Keighley Station is restored to the 1950s/early 60s style which he can remember as a boy. Then he corrects himself and refers to the way it would have looked in that period had it been properly maintained and painted which, of course, is wasn't until he and his fellow members came along.

John has been the Emergency Rostering Officer for Stations and Sales staff since 1984. The Rostering Officer prepares a roster based on availability sheets sent out to staff. John then has the task of filling in gaps and dealing with last minute problems. This can involve contacting staff and asking them to fill positions at short notice.

There is one question which John can't answer. Why does he do it? He was asked this in a recent television interview. He stumbled so badly trying to think of a reason that he was edited out of the programme. Some of us have a sneaking suspicion that he likes railways.

Margaret Jones

Margaret's early railway interest had been limited to her brother's models and to watching the trains pass her school playground just north of Keighley Station during the final years of steam operation. She travelled on the Worth Valley line a few times after reopening.

During the summer of 1976, Margaret decided that her husband, Keith, might benefit from a new leisure interest so she brought him along to Haworth to see what were the possibilities. They both liked what they saw, so they joined the Society straight away. Keith volunteered to work in Haworth shop the following Saturday. He then attended a meeting of the Sales Committee and was immediately appointed Secretary of it.

Before she had time to wonder where this was going to leave her, Margaret decided to dive in herself.

Over the ensuing 15 years, Keith has served a variety of operating and administrative functions, many but not quite all at the same time. He has been a responsible officer, guard and signalman and has been both Chairman and Secretary of the Management Committee. He has been the rostering officer for operating crews and has organised railtours (BR charter trains) in the days when the Society got involved with these.

For her part, Margaret has worked in both sales and buffets. She is rostered as booking clerk and as level crossing keeper, as well as kitchen slave on wine & dine trains.

Margaret as station foreman at Haworth. Will she reach any higher? *(Martin Bairstow)*

When I was appointed Treasurer of the Society in 1980, Keith volunteered to take charge of the sales and buffet accounts, a job which I had done for the previous Treasurer, Ralph Ingham. After two years Margaret took over the function. She must have more stamina than me because she is still doing it after my 'retirement'. This means that Margaret and Keith are opening their house to the mountains of railway waste paper which invades the privacy of members who do work at home.

According to her notes, Margaret has 'slept in some exciting places for the benefit of the Railway!' She is referring to the period when she and Keith were in charge of exhibitions. This is a joint sales/publicity exercise at events such as the Great Yorkshire Show and at such venues as model railway exhibitions. The Rochdale Model Railway Show takes place in February. With a forecast of snow, they decided not to risk leaving it until Saturday morning but to take the van full of stock on Friday evening. They arrived at Rochdale too late to get in. Margaret woke up in her sleeping bag in the early hours laid length ways on the front seat of the transit van in a carpark in Rochdale with snowflakes falling gently but persistently a few inches from her face.

Having a mainly indoor office job, Margaret prefers to be outdoors on the Railway. She is not too keen on meetings and paperwork, but realises that 'behind the scenes' work has to be done in order that members may enjoy the railway. She prefers black engines including the 4F, 8F and the 'Standard' (75078), but can put up with 'Big Jim', the S160 from Poland.

Margaret has typed a number of my book manuscripts, including the present one. It is most helpful to have the support of somebody with more than a little railway experience.

Damian Mills

It has been suggested, quite wrongly, that railway preservation might begin to dwindle or die when it can no longer rely on the generations who can actually remember the age of steam. If there were any truth in this theory then the decline would have set in years ago because one really needs to have been born before 1950 to have other than childhood recollections of railways as they were before everything changed.

Fortunately the Railway continues to attract new members of all age groups. It serves as a measure of just how much time has passed that there are now a number of working members who are younger than the Railway.

Damian Mills was born in Keighley in October 1968 a few months after the re-opening. His first trip on the Worth Valley was on a Santa Special hauled by 'Evening Star' which must have been at Christmas 1973 or 1974. He joined the Society in 1980. He became involved with the Vintage Carriages Trust serving in their shop at Keighley and attending exhibitions on behalf of both the VCT and the KWVR Sales Department. In due course he became the shop manager and was a Committee member of the VCT during the planning stage of the Ingrow Carriage Museum.

Damian is interested in local history of which the Railway is an essential part. However he does not want it merely as a museum piece but wishes to see its continued development playing a role in the present day economy of the area – mainly in the context of tourism. He wants the Railway to be successful commercially.

Damian is a member of a number of other railway organisations, including the Class 40 Society which has two locomotives on the East Lancashire Railway. He joined the Friends of the Settle-Carlisle Line to support what was hopefully the last major anti-closure campaign.

In the early 1980s he made extensive use of West Yorkshire day rover tickets in order to visit various railway installations within and just outside the County.

He has no immediate aspirations to assume any operating position on the Railway. He is content with his VCT work. To date he has steered clear of involvement in Worth Valley politics. He decided that he would attend a monthly Council meeting in April 1990 to see whether this side of the business appealed to him. He duly turned up at the Globe Inn to find that this was the one occasion when the venue had been changed to the Victoria Hotel in order to accommodate members of the Bahamas Locomotive Society who had come to discuss their move to Ingrow. Damian stayed at the Globe and had a drink.

'West Country' 4-6-2 No 34092 'City of Wells' between GN Junction and Ingrow. Built in 1949, this locomotive saw only 15 years use on British Railways. It came to the Worth Valley via Barry Scrapyard. Since 1980 it has worked both on the Worth Valley and on the main line.
(Martin Bairstow)

'Jubilee' 4-6-0 No 45596 'Bahamas', seen between Haworth and Oxenhope, came to the Worth Valley in 1990 when the lease expired on its previous home at Dinting. *(John Sagar)*

0-6-2T No 1054 was built by the London & North Western Railway in 1888. It arrived in the Worth Valley with the 'Bahamas' Collection but had made an earlier visit in 1986. It is seen near GN Junction on the evening of 14 June 1986. *(John Sagar)*

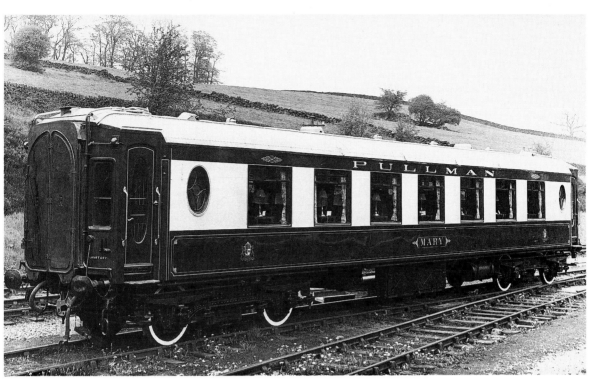

Exterior and interior views of Pullman car 'Mary' (BR Car No. 84, built 1930), now used on Worth Valley 'White Rose Pullman' 'wine & dine' trains. *(K. Roberts)*

Operating Difficulties

Sometimes things go wrong. The following are two tales from my days as a guard on the KWVR.

The second week of July 1976 I took as holiday from work. I was rostered for the normal midweek service on the Railway, four return trips each afternoon with an extra one on the Wednesday morning. The driver all week was Robin Higgins and the fireman Chris Hulme. The loco was No 41241.

On the Tuesday we took four coaches for the first trip at 12.35 from Oxenhope and 13.20 from Keighley – always the busiest – then dropped down to three. On our second arrival at Oxenhope at 15.15, the driver telephoned the Responsible Officer, Graham Mitchell, to report that the front half of the grate had fallen in and No 41241 could only shunt the carriages into the loop then return to Haworth shed.

There was nobody passed to drive the diesel locomotive No D0226 but inside Oxenhope Shed, Basil Hancock was painting railbus No 79962. He travelled with us in the cab of 41241 back to Haworth Yard and started up the other railbus No 79964. It wasn't in the best of health. Once under way I had to keep feeding it water. You do this from inside the vehicle but with some difficulty when carrying double the seating capacity of 56 passengers.

We left Haworth Station for Keighley at 15.56 only 20 minutes late but with such a load that I had to board the vehicle from the far side in order to reach my plastic container of water destined for the cooling system. In those days the smaller stations were request stops and we probably missed them all. We were actually away from Keighley again at 16.10 – five minutes before the booked departure time because there were still crowds at Oxenhope waiting for a train which ought to have gone at 15.30. We reached them at 16.25. There were far too many for us to carry but Graham Mitchell had arranged for them to form two orderly queues; one for Haworth and one for Keighley. We departed at 16.26 with the Haworth passengers, returning immediately so that the Keighley people were away from Oxenhope just ten minutes later.

On our next return, Graham produced strawberries and cream for the driver and myself. He had also by the time found a replacement guard for the final trip so that I could lock up the coaches which has been abandoned in Oxenhope loop.

We were back the next day, but with 4F No 43924 instead.

We started out with No. 41241 and three coaches. In this view taken on 3 April 1976, the second vehicle is the miniature buffet car which had been part of a diesel multiple unit.
(Peter Hutchinson)

We finished up having to convey all the passengers on No. 79964.
(John Bateman)

Saturday 17 March 1979 was the day that Penmanshiel Tunnel collapsed on the East Coast Main Line. An adverse weather forecast had evidently reached Ken Tune in Dronfield who telephoned on Friday evening to ask if I would cover his Saturday morning guard's turn as he did not think that he could get to Haworth. In those days I didn't have a car and my normal method of reaching this duty would have involved taking my bicycle on the train to Keighley then riding to Haworth. The outlook did not look too promising. However further telephone calls revealed that Chris Smyth was in residence at 3 Mill Hey, Haworth and was proposing to take the 9.20 to Keighley, changing there onto the 9.43 for Carlisle. Chris volunteered to set off a little earlier so as to take charge of the diesel railbus from Haworth Yard via Oxenhope Station and down to Keighley where I would take over for the 9.50 departure, having arrived by the same Nottingham to Glasgow train which he was to join. It seemed a perfect solution.

Next morning it was time to put the theory into practice. I trudged through the snow to New Pudsey Station. There was no problem getting into Leeds but the 9.20 to Glasgow was running 2½ hours late. All I could do was go for the 9.35 local and they would just have to wait for me a Keighley. I was joined by Max Burgess, a Worth Valley signalman.

Platform 4 at Keighley was deserted and the tracks covered in virgin snow. The telephones worked and we learned that the diesel railbus had been blocked in Haworth Yard by a steam loco which was frozen up. Oil fired 'Brussels' had been lit up and would be coming as soon as possible. In the meantime would Max and I care to dig out the points at Keighley then walk to Damems and free the level crossing.

We did all this up to our knees in snow in places as we walked up the line taking care to step on the sleepers when we crossed bridges. We cleared Damems crossing in time to open the gates for 'Brussels' and its two coach train running about 2½ hours late. It was well laden with members armed with shovels and other snow clearing equipment. Also lurking in the guards van was Chris Smyth. On arrival at Keighley he walked casually over the footbridge onto platform 2 where he had just a couple of minutes to wait before boarding the Nottingham-Glasgow, also 2½ hours late.

Both these stories have a happy ending but they also have a moral. It wasn't the loco breaking down or the snow which stopped the service. It was the failure to train all drivers on the stand-by diesel and the illegal parking of an engine.

'Brussels' in charge of the 14.50 Keighley to Oxenhope about ½ mile short of its destination on 29 March 1975. This loco, purchased direct from the Longmoor Military Railway in 1971, will eventually revert to coal firing.
(Peter Hutchinson)

The Vintage Carriages Trust

By Michael Cope

A major aspect in the early days of the revived Worth Valley Railway was a severe shortage of money. In this circumstance, the intial passenger coaches for use on the Railway were acquired (or hired) from whatever source was cheap. The result was that the re-opening train was far from characteristic of a Midland branch line, consisting as it did of two privately-owned Pullman cars ('Zena' and Car No 84, now 'Mary'), two of the available three ex-Metropolitan Railway high capacity coaches, and a brake coach built to a South Eastern & Chatham design by the then very young Southern Railway. Of these, all but the Pullman cars had been purchased privately for an earlier but abortive Preservation scheme—the Westerham Valley Railway. The three Metropolitan coaches and the 'Chatham Brake' went on to become the mainstay of Worth Valley coaching stock in the first few years of operation.

Also in those early days, a small group for Worth Valley members became very much aware that historic four—and six-wheeled coaches (by that stage surviving only in Engineers' trains) were rapidly disappearing. United under the banner of the Vintage Carriages Trust, this small group first purchased one such coach, identified as DE940281E and based at Boston. It arrived on the Railway in June 1966. Although superficially in rather a run-down state, this six-wheeled former Great Northern Railway Brake Third of 1888 was basically solid, being withdrawn from British Railways service only because the Guard's door had been broken off.

The cost was £60: about six weeks' wages at the time. External restoration to original varnished teak livery was successfully finished by VCT members within quite a short time.

One member of the group had already purchased privately a rather dilapidated Stores Van, DE953003, from the Engineers' train at Retford. This stripped-out four-wheeled vehicle had been built as a tri-composite passenger coach (one First, one Second, two Third Class and a central luggage compartment) as long ago as 1876 by the Manchester, Sheffield and Lincolnshire Railway. It arrived at Haworth in March 1965—more than three years before the re-opening. Subsequently this vehicle was transferred to the embryonic VCT.

Pursuing the theme of saving historic passenger stock, the VCT next purchased the ex-Midland Railway clerestory coach then identified as DM195955. It is perhaps best to say that it was not the preferred choice —a similar vehicle, at Lancaster Green Ayre, was missed. The coach actually obtained came 'sight unseen' from Derby and, from the restoration point of view, was definitely a mistake. However, it saw useful employment as Worth Valley volunteers' accommodation at Haworth (the celebrated 'Midland Mansions') before being passed to the Midland Railway Centre at Butterley as a long-term restoration project.

The VCT's present collection of historic four and six wheeled carriages was completed by the purchase of a third ex-Departmental vehicle, DM284677. This had been built in Derby in 1886 as a Midland Railway six-

'Sir Berkeley' passing Oakworth with a freight on 26 March 1968 during filming for the BBC version of 'The Railway Children'.
(John S. Whiteley)

wheeled composite, having two First, two Third class and a central luggage compartment. When found it was in use as a store by the Signal & Telegraph Engineer under cover within Liverpool Edge Hill Locomotive Shed. It arrived at Haworth in 1968.

For a few years, the Trust had a custodial agreement with the Gresley Society concerning E16520E. This is an LNER third class brake end side corridor coach, built in York in 1939. It had come to the Railway in July 1965, in company with the Gresley Society's LNER Buffet and Observation Cars and N2 locomotive 4744. Sadly, the Worth Valley Railway's operating need for high-capacity coaches, weight restrictions and other problems meant that this coach and the rest of the Gresley Society's collection had little opportunity for use on the Railway. All left the Worth Valley in late 1978 following the Gresley Society's decision to relocate on the Great Central Railway at Loughborough.

Meantime, the Railway had re-opened. The three Metropolitan coaches and the Chatham were very heavily used in the first year or two of the Society's operation. They were then to a great extent supplanted by more modern British Railways Standard Mark I coaches, which needed much less maintenance. The Trust was able to help the Railway at this time by purchasing two of these Standard coaches—E48007 and E46228, which arrived in early 1969. These had both been built in 1955, the former at Doncaster and the latter at Derby. Both served their purpose reasonably well but in due course their condition deteriorated irretrievably. E48007 was sold to the Somerset & Dorset Railway Circle in 1973. Their intended preservation scheme at Radstock proved abortive, and this coach was eventually scrapped in Glasgow in 1976. E46228 was withdrawn from Worth Valley service in September 1975. With most of its body scrapped it saw some further use on the Railway as runner for the Grafton steam crane. The frames were scrapped at Ingrow in 1983, with the bogies still in use on the Railway under sleeping car E2521.

The VCT was able to assist the Railway in up-dating the coaching fleet by the purchase of E14695, which arrived at Haworth (from Bishops Stortford) in 1969.

This was a gangwayed centre corridor Open Second built by British Railways in 1951 to a Southern Railway design by O V S Bulleid. It was intended very much as a working coach for use on the Railway, and to complement the 'Chatham'. This purchase brought the Trust's fleet of historic coaches to four: the Victorian MS&L, Midland and Great Northern coaches, and the much more recent Bulleid.

Sadly, very little beyond the above was recorded by the Vintage Carriages Trust in its early days. Only a very small number of members were involved. They all had other jobs on the Railway and were 'doers' rather than 'recorders'. As the Trust's fleet of coaches expanded, the 'doing' made it increasingly important to have a source of finance for restoration and repair work. From the earliest days, the Trust had been selling second-hand books, lamps, station signs, and all manner of other railwayana. Initially this was by post, from an address in North London. Later, there was also a stall in the Waiting Room on Platform Four at Keighley Station. This soon moved to the office at the end of the platform, formerly used by the BR Gas Fitting Department. The Trust has now operated this 'Platform Four Relics Shop' for well over twenty years. Only much more recently has this little shop been complemented by the Railway Relic Shop at 5 Mill Hey, Haworth—conveniently close to the station.

With much hard work, the sales activities have provided an income sufficient to sustain a programme of work on the fleet of historic coaches. The first full restoration undertaken was the 'Chatham'. Over the years, the water tank above the toilet compartment had moved relative to the bodywork whilst the coach was in motion. This let in water, producing a very nasty attack of wet rot above this and the adjacent passenger compartment. The coach no longer fell within the operating requirements of the Railway. It needed substantial expenditure and there was for a time a very real possibility that it would be scrapped. Happily, after a great deal of discussion, agreement was reached by which VCT purchased this vehicle from the Railway for the nominal sum of one pound. Members of the Trust then rectified the wet-rot damage with the assistance of a

The VCT shop at No. 5 Mill Hey, Haworth.   *(Martin Bairstow)*

contractor, attended to many other matters internally and externally, and repainted the coach in early Southern Railway green livery. This restoration was completed to a high standard in rather less than one year. This was accelerated by something of an ultimatum from the Railway, requiring the 'Chatham' to be available for use in time for the Spring Enthusiasts' Day of 17 March 1973. This was successfully accomplished, although lining and lettering had to wait until later. For some years this coach then formed part of the Worth Valley 'Pullman Train' and was stabled in Oxenhope Exhibition Shed when not in use.

By this stage, the three Metropolitan coaches were no longer in regular use, as they were in need of much remedial work. They no longer fell within the remit of the Worth Valley Carriage & Wagon Department, which had responsibility for providing running coaches for the regular passenger services. This meant, almost exclusively, the easier-to-maintain Mark I vehicles. To ensure the continued preservation of the ex-Metropolitan coaches, the Trust reached agreement with the Railway and with their owner to purchase all three at a price reflecting what the owner had paid, plus an adjustment for inflation.

Encouraged by its success with the 'Chatham', the Trust turned its attention to the Manchester Sheffield & Lincolnshire Railway four wheeler. This project took a little longer: to be precise, fifteen years from 1972 to 1987. Space does not permit the saga to be fully described. Suffice it to say that there was at least one major false start. Work was done on the coach variously by volunteers and by contractors in Bradford, Ingrow, Carnforth and Oxenhope. By the time the work was successfully completed the Trust had gained Charitable status and had joined what is now the Yorkshire & Humberside Museums Council, whose financial and other assistance is gratefully acknowledged. On eventual completion the coach won the Association of Railway Preservation Societies' 1988 'Best Preserved Coach' competition (jointly with the North Norfolk Railway's Gresley Buffet Car). Despite the setbacks, the excessive time taken, and experience gained the hard way, the Trust is justifiably proud of its very successful restoration of this vehicle—now resplendent in early Great Central livery as No 176.

Other major restoration projects have also taken many years to complete. Work on the nine compartment Third Class Metropolitan occupied twelve years. The seven compartment First Class is taking a little longer, at sixteen years to date. These extended timescales are by no means uncommon: elsewhere on the Worth Valley Railway, other historic coaches (not owned by the Trust) are at the time of writing in their seventeenth and their eighteenth years of restoration. These experiences surely must serve as a warning to anyone about to embark on restoration of any historic railway carriage (or, worse, carriage body) without access to good facilities, good experience—and lots of time and money.

With the benefit of hindsight, the 1960s and 1970s saw many lost opportunities to form a top-quality and representative collection of historic coaches on the Worth Valley Railway. This now seems regrettable, but was perhaps inevitable. The Railway just did not have the space to allow Vintage Carriages Trust (or any other Society or individual) to collect historic coaches additional to those already present on the Railway, no matter how historically important they might be. Also the Railway was—and in its own right still is—very much concerned with the business of efficiently and reliably transporting passengers from one end of the Worth Valley Branch to the other. There was no way in which the somewhat stretched time and money (and space) could be extended to allow the luxury of collecting further historic coaches. The result is the geographically unbalanced present collection of the Trust. Hopefully in years to come exchanges with, or acquisitions from, other collections may allow a more comprehensive display showing the development of the railway carriage.

These days its choice of name is a slight embarrassment for the Vintage Carriages Trust as it now owns three small, interesting and ancient steam locomotives. These are: 'Bellerophon', an 0-6-0WT built in 1874 at Haydock Colliery; 'Sir Berkeley', an 0-6-0ST contractor's locomotive built in 1891 by Manning Wardle of Leeds; and 'Lord Mayor' of 1893, again a contractor's locomotive built in Leeds, but this time an 0-4-0ST by Hudswell, Clarke & Company. Apart from their extreme age, their main characteristic is that they are of no use whatsoever to the Railway for the practical (and absolutely essential) business of running revenue-earning passenger trains. They are however of very considerable historic importance. As with the historic coaches, these locomotives need the support of a group removed from the mainstream activity of running the Railway. With its successful record of carriage preservation, the Trust emerged as the alternative body best able to guarantee this support.

'Bellerophon' was donated to the Worth Valley Society by the National Coal Board North Western Area (as the eventual successors to Richard Evans' Haydock Collieries) in 1966. Sadly, the locomotive as received at Haworth was in very run down condition. Its small size and antiquity denied it a place in the Railway's working fleet. The very best that could lie ahead for the locomotive was as a static exhibit. As such, 'Bellerophon' spent many a long year exposed to the elements at the buffer stops in Haworth Yard. However, as early as summer 1973 the first of several correspondents called in the Society's magazine *Push & Pull* for the restoration to full working order of 'Bellerophon'. These various challenges were taken up by the VCT. The Trust formally purchased the locomotive from the Railway, for the token sum of again one pound. Then, with the aid of a generous grant from the Fund for the Conservation and Preservation of Historic Material (administered by the Science Museum), with a great deal of hard work from within the Trust and thanks to donations from many people, the impossible was achieved. After some four years effort, 'Bellerophon' was steamed again in May 1985.

This veteran locomotive has continued in active use. Although capable of hauling a much greater load—given sufficient time and frequent watering—'Bellerophon' has to be limited to a two-coach train when running within the normal Worth Valley timetable. Operating as a relief train in the off-season timetable has proved very popular, albeit of necessity rather an infrequent pleasure. 'Bellerophon' has also travelled widely since restoration, including visits to the Bluebell Railway, Carnforth, Crewe, Eggborough and Padiham Power Stations, Embsay, Manchester Liverpool Road and the Middleton and Swanage Railways. At all these locations, 'Bellerophon' has behaved very well and has indeed made a great number of friends. Hopefully, such travels will continue for many years to come.

The transformation of 'Bellerophon' from a derelict hulk has been formally recognised by a Transport Trust 'Commendation', a National Coal Board 'Steam Heritage Award', and an Institution of Mechanical Engineers' Heritage Hallmarks Scheme 'Blue Plaque'.

The rather picturesque Manning Wardle 0-6-0 saddletank Sir Berkeley' was an early arrival at Haworth in 1965, having been purchased from the Cranford Ironstone Company by Mr Roger Crombleholme. After a deal of work, 'Sir Berkeley' first steamed again some three years later. Occasional filming and other special appearances followed, including a role in the BBC version of *"The Railway Children".* However, by the early 1980s 'Sir Berkeley' had been out of use for some time and needed a great deal of attention. As a way forward, the Vintage Carriages Trust acquired the locomotive from Mr Crombleholme for a purely token sum. With the very helpful assistance of the Science Museum's Conservation Fund and (later) of the Yorkshire & Humberside Museums Council, the Trust embarked on what has turned out to be a full rebuild of the locomotive. This has proved a very protracted exercise. A succession of members in turn have led the project. One moved out of the area whilst another died at a tragically early age. Further health problems have dogged progress but a determined effort is being made to achieve steaming during 'Sir Berkeley's' centenary year in 1991.

'Lord Mayor' has been on the Railway since June 1968. This diminutive locomotive has been steamed from time to time, but in recent years became very much a static exhibit pending resolution of ownership. Following somewhat complex negotiations and with the assistance of generous donations from a small number of its members, the VCT gained full ownership fo 'Lord Mayor' in 1990. The Trust's intention is to restore 'Lord Mayor' to allow steaming in its centenary year of 1993.

Over the years, the Vintage Carriages Trust had become all too aware of the supreme importance of undercover accommodation for historic wooden-bodied coaches. This applies especially to the Pennine winters of the Worth Valley. The Trust has a long-standing agreement with the Worth Valley Railway for the use of 120 feet of covered accommodation at Oxenhope. However, with severe pressure on covered space— whether for locomotives, for coaches on display, or for those undergoing maintenance or restoration—it was inevitable that some had to be left outside. The resultant deterioration created the classic 'one step forward, two backwards' situation. Therefore the Trust resolved that it would, if at all possible, build its own Carriage Shed.

There were two major problems. The first was finance; the second was location. The Worth Valley is fast running out of available space. A Carriage Shed needs a great deal of this, not only for the Shed itself, but also for the necessary connection to the rest of the Railway. A site immediately beside the existing Museum building at Oxenhope was considered. This would have necessitated the culverting of the stream running beside that Museum, with a narrow single-road Shed built above this to provide a rather basic shelter for the three Metropolitan coaches. However, the cost and complexity of this project, together with its limited benefits, resulted

Work in progress on the 'Chatham' coach inside the Vintage Carriage Museum at Ingrow. The next vehicle is the Great Central tri-composite No 176.   *(John Sagar)*

in a decision not to proceed at this site.

After a great deal of consideration, the decision was made to build the Carriage Shed at Ingrow. Here, the station project had recently been completed. The station yard however was derelict, containing but one isolated siding. To build something worthwhile here was a major challenge. Now is not the time to list all the problems, the agonising, the aggravations, and all the other difficulties brought on by this decision. It would be easy to say: 'If we were to start again, we wouldn't do it that way'. However, we can say: "The Trust was successful in its project, and has opened and is now operating the very worthwhile Ingrow Carriage Museum".

Certainly this is by far the most important project yet undertaken by the Trust. Its achievement is primarily that an assured future has been given to the majority of the collection, by the very fact that the building provides good protection from the weather and an environment in which continuing restoration and conservation work can be undertaken. Equally importantly, the Trust is now able to show its collection to a wider public, with the possibility of much better display and interpretation. The building has progressed from a 'Carriage Shed' to 'The Ingrow Carriage Museum'.

Finance for the project was a major problem. With the Trust's previous substantial achievements, and with the change of emphasis from a 'Shed' to a 'Museum', it is pleasing to acknowledge with gratitude the financial and other support received from the Museums & Galleries Commission, from the English Tourist Board, from Bradford Metropolitan District Council—and from more than eight hundred individual persons, by way of donations and loans. Certainly, without all this support the project would not have been possible.

It was with very great pleasure that members of the Trust heard that VCT, jointly with the Worth Valley Railway, had won the Association of Railway Preservation Societies' 1990 Annual Award. This was given 'for successful and practical development of Ingrow station and yard to include homes for the Vintage Railway Carriage Museum and the Bahamas Locomotive Society'.

The Ingrow Carriage Museum is open at least from noon to 4pm every Saturday and Sunday throughout the year and daily during the summer. The Shop at 5 Mill Hey has similar opening times whilst that on Platform 4 at Keighley is usually open whenever Worth Valley trains are running. The Trust is always pleased to welcome new members, either as working members or as supporters: please enquire at the Museum or at either of the two Shops, or write to: The Secretary, VCT: c/o The Railway Station, Haworth Keighley, West Yorkshire BD22 8NJ.

'Lord Mayor' peeping out of the Vintage Carriage Museum at Ingrow.

(Martin Bairstow)

On and off the Railway

Written Jointly with Philippa Simpson

There are now something like 100 preserved railways of one sort or another in the United Kingdom. To an extent they are in competition with each other for members and customers. They are also in competition with other leisure activities upon which the population can spend its time and money.

Despite the scale of the competition, there are a number of factors which weigh heavily in favour of the Worth Valley keeping its position both as one of the country's leading preserved railways and as one of the principal tourist amenities in West Yorkshire.

Firstly it is a complete railway running just as it always did from the main line junction to the branch terminus. Secondly it serves an established tourist area. Many preserved lines are accessible only by car and have little to offer apart from the railway journey itself. The Worth Valley can be reached by train from practically any part of the country. The railway is only part of the day out and so can be used again and again as a means of visiting different attractions or as part of different itineraries.

Why do people come to the Worth Valley?

As already noted, when the line first opened in 1867, the local press quickly observed that it was being used to get people out of the towns into the countryside and on to the moors. This free attraction is still very much available and the Railway is still used as a means of reaching the countryside without a car or even as a means of getting back to where the car is parked after a one way walk.

There is endless scope for walking in and around the Worth Valley including the rail trail which follows close to the line between Oxenhope, Haworth and Oakworth.

This chapter gives a description of some of the museums which can be visited in conjunction with a journey on the Keighley & Worth Valley Railway. There are two museums on the Railway itself. At Oxenhope the green Exhibition Shed houses a number of steam locomotives, the Pullman train and all manner of railwayana. Admission is free to train ticket holders and Society Members. At Ingrow there is the Vintage Carriages Museum described in Michael Cope's article. Here there is a charge for admission—reduced for rail travellers and KWVR Members.

The Brontë Parsonage

The first venture into organised tourism came in 1895 when the Brontë Society opened its first museum. The Rev Patrick Brontë had been the Rector of Haworth from 1820 until 1861. He outlived his three daughters Emily, Charlotte and Anne and also his rather less successful son, Branwell.

In 1928, the Parsonage was purchased for the nation by Sir James Roberts. It was entrusted to the Brontë Society which has attempted as far as possible to recreate its mid-nineteenth century appearance.

The Parsonage is at the top of Haworth village. It can be reached on foot by crossing over the footbridge at the station and then attacking the steep cobbled road which climbs between the park on the left hand side and the Community Centre on the right. You must cross the bypass before joining the Main Street. This is also cobbled, and is full of up market touristy shops selling

The Brontë Parsonage viewed across the Churchyard.
(Martin Bairstow)

lace, chocolates, expensive toys, pots, souvenirs made out of old shuttles and bobbins together with a number of restaurants and cafés.

To reach the Parsonage, turn left by the Tourist Information Centre at the top of the Main Street. Walk past Branwell Brontë's local hostelry, the Black Bull, then by the Church.

The Parsonage is an imposing stone house overlooking the Churchyard, Guide leaflets are available in a number of languages. Inside you visit Mr Brontë's study, simply furnished, where he often took meals alone. Then there is the dining room where the sisters did much of their writing and where Emily Brontë died in 1848 after refusing to admit that she was ill until it was too late.

Still downstairs at the back of the house is Mr Nicholl's study. He was the Curate who married Charlotte Brontë. His study was converted out of a former peat store which had also been used to accommodate the pet geese.

In the kitchen one sees the old range where Emily made bread whilst learning German from books propped up on the table.

Upstairs is Mr Brontë's bedroom adorned by a number of portraits painted by son Branwell. He was the black sheep of the family. His aspirations to become an artist were overtaken by a weakness for drink. He took a job as 'assistant clerk in charge' at Sowerby Bridge Station when the Manchester & Leeds Railway opened in 1840. He was soon promoted to 'clerk in charge' at Luddendenfoot but then was sacked because a porter stole money whilst Branwell went drinking.

One of the exhibits in Branwell's bedroom is the chair which he used when frequenting the Black Bull. Other upstairs rooms includes Charlotte's bedroom with her clothes laid out and her work box. Then there is the servant's room at the back. Mr Brontë did quite well to have at least one servant waiting on him. His origins in County Down were very humble. He had taught himself to read and write.

The Parsonage was enlarged after the Brontë period in 1878. The extension is used to house various exhibitions and a museum shop stocking rare and out of print books as well as the usual mementos.

The Parsonage attracts visitors from all over the World. On one day in August 1990 the visitors' book showed people from Japan, Australia, China, the USA, Italy, Belgium, France, Guatamala, Ireland, Spain, South Korea, the Philippines and all over Britain.

It takes about one hour to go round the Parsonage which is open daily except at Christmas and for a three week winter closure in late January/early February.

Cliffe Castle, Keighley

Built in the early nineteenth century as Cliffe Hall, this property was purchased in 1848 by the Butterfields, a local family who had done well in the textile trade. During the years 1875 to 1884, it was transformed by Henry Isaac Butterfield into a mansion and renamed Cliffe Castle.

In 1950, the Butterfield family sold the property to a local benefactor, Sir Bracewell Smith who entrusted it to Keighley Corporation. It opened as a museum in 1959.

Situated about one mile from Keighley Station along the old Skipton Road, Cliffe Castle can be reached on Sunday afternoons in summer by a minibus service which connects with Worth Valley trains and which is free to holders of KWVR tickets. Cliffe Castle itself is also free.

The Castle is set in its own park which slopes gently upwards from the main road. There are fountains, a band stand, magnificent mature trees, rose gardens and bedding plants providing a blaze of colour in summer.

To the side of the Castle is a self service cafe, children's play area, a cactus house and glass houses containing tropical plants. Close to the cafe are avaries, rabbits and peacocks.

As one enters the Castle, there is a suite of four reception rooms furnished in the style of the French Second Empire. Ebony, brass and gilt abound.

There are a series of permanent exhibitions. 'Airedale — The Formation of a Valley' is a geological exhibition focussing on fossils and minerals found in the area. Centrepiece is a reconstruction of a crocodile like amphibian based on a fossil found in Bradford. The Natural History exhibition comprises a well displayed collection of stuffed animals, birds, fishes and insects depicted in their natural habitats. The minerals section of the museum provides a striking display against a black background of different coloured rocks.

Upstairs the 'Bygone Rooms' offer a display of antiquated kitchenware and household utensils, local pottery, a hive of live honey bees, Victorian toys and musical intruments.

There are also temporary exhibitions. During 1990 these included 'Victorian Values', a series of paintings from the Bradford City Council Collection, Quilt Art, Mill Life and Birds.

A visit can easily occupy two hours. There is something for everyone.

East Riddlesden Hall, Keighley

This National Trust property is found in a very attractive setting about one mile from Keighley Station on the old main road towards Bingley. It is served by frequent buses as well as the 'Scenic Minibus' on summer Sunday afternoons.

The Hall was rebuilt in the seventeenth century by James Murgatroyd, a wealthy if slightly disreputable clothier from Halifax. The 120 foot Great Barn is older being a survivor from the earlier Medieval Hall. This now houses a collection of farm carts and implements.

From the main gate, the Hall is seen across a large pond surrounded by trees and frequented by hungry ducks, food for whom may be purchased at the shop.

The visitor enters the house through a two-storey porch with a unique circular window above. Panelled rooms with fine plasterwork and mullioned windows provide an ideal setting for collections of pewter, domestic utensils and Yorkshire Oak Furniture.

Thanks to the neglect of a succession of absentee landlords in the nineteenth century, East Riddlesden has remained largely unaltered from pre-industrial times. It was rescued from threatened development in the 1930s by twin brothers William and John Brigg who gave it to the National Trust in 1934.

The Hall is open Easter to October. There are special events outside this period such as a 'Costume Weekend' and 'Christmas Music in the Great Barn'.

Even out of season, the National Trust shop and a rather civilised tea room are open at weekends in the former bothy. The adjacent pig sty has been commandeered as a toilet block.

The Haworth Museum of Childhood

When we arrived at the Museum in West Street beyond the top of the Main Street, we found a 'For Sale' board on the property. The explanation was that they were looking for more suitable premises in the centre of the village, so we do not know where it may be next year.

The Museum comprises a selection of toys dating from the nineteenth century up to fairly recent times. Centre piece are the seven working model railway layouts. These come in various gauges and in varying degrees of authenticity. In general the older the vintage, the less the concern that it should conform faithfully to the real thing. Some of the 1920s specimens are period pieces in their own right without necessarily being based on any real life prototype.

Other displays include dolls and dolls houses spanning a period of a century with a good collection of foreign costumes. These are puppets, cuddly toys, Meccano and Bako kits, Dinky toys and an old record player.

The Museum is open 10.30am to 5.30pm daily from April to October and at weekends November to March. It takes about half an hour to go round.

Bygone Days, Haworth

This memorabilia museum is located in Belle Isle Road which runs parallel to the railway, below the Central Park and above Haworth goods yard. It is reached by the footbridge from the Station.

Behind the façade which resembles something between a chapel and a cinema, is a recreation of an old street. There is a toy shop with a model train in operation, a chemist's shop and post office. Outside the garage are a number of motor bikes including one with a side car whose claim to fame is that it was patronised by Nora Batty in 'Last of the Summer Wine' – just one of a number of exhibits which have found a television role.

The Museum is on two levels. Above the ground floor shops which front onto the cobbled square is a balcony serving further shops selling sweets, hardware and ironmongery. Afternoon tea may be taken in the Old Court Cafe.

Bygone Days is open 11am to 5pm at weekends all year and on Wednesdays and Thursdays April to October. Allow at least half an hour to get round.

Ex-L&Y 0-6-0 ST No 752 pulling away from Oakworth on 28 March 1982. Built in 1881, No 752 began life as a tender engine similar to No 52044 but was rebuilt in 1898.

(D. J. Fowler)

A New Order in Airedale and Wharfedale

'Pacers' have brought a faster and more frequent service since 1987. 144013 enters Bingley Station from Leeds.
(John Bateman)

Railways Through Airedale and Wharfedale was published in this series in 1985. It sold out during 1990 and a new edition will be considered to celebrate electrification in about 1994. In the meantime what follows is a resumé of recent events on the lines which connect with the Worth Valley branch.

By the time of the Worth Valley reopening in 1968, the fortunes of the neighbouring lines in Airedale and Wharfedale had reached something of a low ebb. Many local stations had closed in 1965. The hourly Bradford to Skipton trains had been halved in frequency and cut short at Keighley. In 1968 even this service became the subject of a formal closure proposal along with a renewed attempt to eliminate the remaining lines into Wharfedale and to close Bradford Forster Square. The (almost) hourly trains from Leeds to Skipton would then have been the only passenger service in the area but a shadow loomed even over this.

The 1967 White Paper published by the then Transport Secretary, Barbara Castle, may now be seen as having been a step towards stabilising the size of the BR network. But that document suggested that Leeds-Skipton should be freight only.

As if to emphasise that the route survived only on a stop gap basis, nobody was prepared to do anything about the crazy situation at Shipley where trains had to shunt for want of a platform on the main line curve. Historically this had not mattered because there was so much traffic coming out of Bradford to give Shipley a service in all directions.

Events almost took a disastrous turn in August 1972

when the Transport Secretary finally pronounced judgement on the Bradford to Keighley service which was to close. Bradford-Ilkley was to operate only five times a day with a ten minute detour via Apperley Junction, but Leeds-Ilkley was reprieved.

In a move which was then without precedent Bradford Council stepped in with a subsidy to keep things as they were. Other authorities which were to make up the future Metropolitan City of Bradford quickly announced that they would share the burden. Baildon Urban District Council did so on condition that its station, closed in 1953, should be reopened.

The West Yorkshire Passenger Transport Executive came into being on 1 April 1974 and immediately assumed an interest in the local rail system. This was formalised in 1977 by an agreement under Section 20 of the 1968 Transport Act by which the Executive contracts for BR to provide a particular level of service and meets the revenue shortfall.

With the May 1978 timetable change most trains from Leeds to Skipton and from Leeds and Bradford to Ilkley were put back onto an hourly interval pattern. The following year saw the Bradford to Keighley service almost quadrupled to a half hourly interval during most of the day. At last, also in 1979, an additional platform was brought into use at Shipley on the Leeds to Skipton curve. A year later the signalling and track layout was altered to permit trains in the opposite direction also to use the new platform thereby finally eliminating the shunting operation.

Station closures during the 1960s had left a situation where the PTE was subsidising trains which ran through ut did not serve some quite significant communities. Crossflatts opened in May 1982. There had never been a station there previously. Saltaire followed in April 1984 on the same site as the structure which had been demolished following closure in 1965.

There then followed a temporary setback. From October 1985, the Bradford-Keighley service went down to hourly whilst most Bradford-Ilkley trains were stopped short at Guiseley, through passengers changing onto a train from Leeds. Some people predicted that the local rail network would collapse with the abolition of the County Council but in April 1986 control of the PTE passed to a joint board made up of representatives from the five Metropolitan Districts. Little time was lost in publishing a 'rail plan' which secured the future of all routes within West Yorkshire.

With the introduction of new rolling stock, frequencies have been improved . Leeds-Skipton became half hourly on Saturdays from May 1987 and on every weekday a year later. The hourly Bradford-Ilkley service was restored in May 1988 when Leeds-Ilkley became half hourly on Saturdays. For May 1990 the hourly Bradford to Keighley train was extended to Skipton whilst Leeds-Ilkley became half hourly every weekday.

At one time Sunday travel was virtually impossible but now all stations are served at about half the weekday frequency. Further stations have re-opened at Frizinghall, Steeton & Silsden and Cononley. The last named is outside the PTE area but fortunately could be dealt with relatively cheaply as the platforms had not been demolished.

In June 1990, Bradford Forster Square Station was resited as part of a proposed retail development. The new station is equipped to handle 'Inter City' trains. It is hoped that there will be up to six through London trains after electrification. There is also a possibility that direct services to the Continent may start from Bradford.

The PTE electric plan for Airedale and Wharfedale envisages frequencies of at least two trains per hour on all five routes: Leeds-Bradford, Leeds-Skipton, Leeds-Ilkley, Bradford-Skipton and Bradford-Ilkley. This would give a 15 minute interval service each way through Keighley whilst Shipley station should see at least 16 departures per hour.

The Airedale line is more than just a commuter route from Leeds and Bradford to Skipton. There remains what we used to call the Morecambe line but this is in the doldrums. It is possible that it may soon offer only four trains daily from Leeds to Lancaster - not necessarily even through to Morecambe.

The main outlet beyond Skipton was via the Settle & Carlisle Line, opened in 1876 to give the Midland Railway direct access to Scotland. Condemned in the Beeching Report, the route lingered on but by the early 1980s it appeared doomed. Then it became the subject of what will hopefully have been the last major closure controversy. This dragged on for nearly eight years. Each time BR mishandled the situation the resultant publicity caused an increase in traffic until, finally, in April 1989, the Transport Secretary announced that it would remain open.

There are currently six trains each way between Leeds and Carlisle. All stop at Keighley, thus providing a direct link between what some people describe as England's most scenic main line and what others consider to be its best preserved branch line.

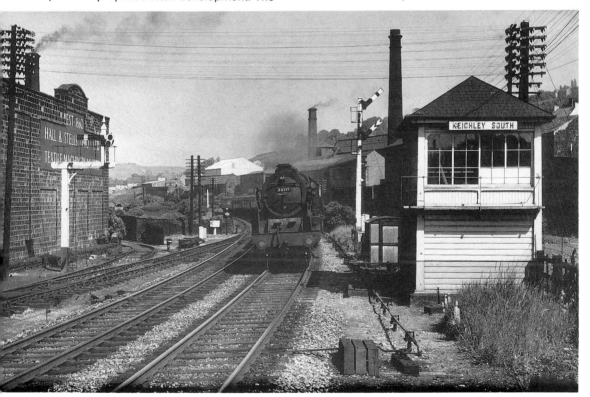

The old order in Airedale, 'Royal Scot' class No. 46117 'Welsh Guardsman' passing Keighley South Box in May 1957 possibly with an afternoon Leeds–Morecambe.   *(A. M. Ross)*

A Carlisle to Leeds service formed of a three coach 156 arrives at Saltaire in February 1991. The re-opened station is in superior style to the average PTE halt. *(Martin Bairstow)*

A station which the author would particularly like to see come back to life. Apperley Bridge in September 1964, just six months before closure. *(Geoffrey Lewthwaite)*